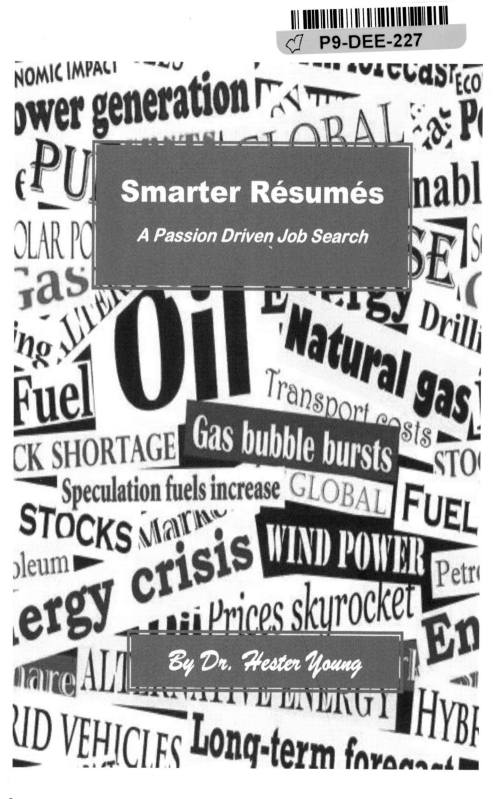

Smarter Résumés

A Passion Driven Job Search

By Dr. Hester Young

Smarter Résumés

A Passion Driven Job Search

By

Hester Young, BS, MA, EdD

A Progress Publication

A Ministry Outreach of James and Dr. Hester Young

JUL   2013

5

Smarter Résumés: A Passion Driven Job Search

Unless otherwise indicated, all Scripture quotations are taken from the NIV.

Smarter Résumés

A Passion Driven Job Search

First Edition by Dr. Hester Young

All copyrights Reserved © by Dr. Hester Young
2012 Library of Congress

ISBN-13: 978-1470079925
ISBN-10: 1470079925

Dr. Hester Young
P.O. Box 59103
Summerville, SC   29485

Email: SmarterRésumés@yahoo.com
Web site: SmarterRésumés.com

Printed in the U.S.A.

Jeremiah 29:11 (NIV)

[11] For I know the plans I have for you," declares the LORD, "plans to prosper you and not to harm you, plans to give you hope and a future.

DEDICATION

This book is dedicated to the hundreds of students that I have counseled, mentored, and served. You have taught me how to create meaningful resources to advance student services within an undergraduate environment.

Smarter Résumés: A Passion Driven Job Search

CONTENTS

INTRODUCTION

Welcome to the realistic world of career planning. The goal of this book is to encourage individuals to understand their strengths, explore and gather occupational information, make decisions, set goals and take action. Let's begin by defining the term, "Career Planning." Career Planning is a lifelong process, which includes choosing an occupation, getting a job, growing in our job, possibly changing careers, and eventually retiring. It involves a series of steps to help facilitate your journey of finding purpose-driven employment. I want you to discover your interests, skills, personality traits, Investigate career choices, options, and opportunities available to you, and setting goals to pursue employment. Some people hate to do it. Some love to do it. Some go to great lengths to avoid doing it. Some do it too much. While there are many different attitudes toward work, one thing remains constant: work must be done. Since the Garden of Eden everyone has worked or depended on someone else's work for their survival. Work sets a person's lifestyle—where you live, when you sleep and eat, the time with family, even your dress. It is important to assess yourself to be sure that you are meeting your goals. By the end of this book you should be able to answer the following questions:

- What do I like to do?

- What activities do I find fun, motivating, interesting and enjoyable?
- What skills and abilities do I have or want to develop?
- What personal style or characteristics do I have that are important to me in the work place?
- What purpose or goal do I want to accomplish in my career?
- How did you get started in this career?
- What is a typical day like?
- What type of training or education is required?
- What are the starting and average salaries?

Chapter 1
PERSONAL BRAND

Chapter 1

PERSONAL BRAND

Look for Exciting New Occupations in the 21st Century

New occupations for the 21st Century and beyond will center on information, energy, high-tech, healthcare, and financial industries. They promise to create a new occupational structure and vocabulary relating to computers, robotics, biotechnology, lasers, and fiber optics. And as these fields begin to apply new technologies to developing new innovations, they in  turn will generate other new occupations in the 21st century. While most new occupations are not major growth fields, because they do not initially generate a large number of new jobs, they will present individuals with fascinating new opportunities to become leaders in pioneering new fields and industries.

Futurists identify several emerging occupations for the coming decades. Most tend to brainstorm lists of occupational titles they feel will emerge in the next decade based on present trends. Others identify additional occupations which may be created from new, unforeseen technological breakthroughs. Several are listed below.

- artificial intelligence technician
- aqua culturist
- automotive fuel cell battery technician
- benefits analyst
- bionic electron technician
- computational linguist
- computer microprocessor
- cryonics technician
- dialysis technologist
- electronic mail technician
- fiber optic technician
- fusion engineer
- hazardous waste technician
- horticultural therapy
- image consultant
- information broker
- information center manager
- job developer
- leisure consultant
- materials utilization specialist
- medical diagnostic imaging technician
- myotherapist
- relocation counselor
- retirement counselor
- robot technician
- shyness consultant
- software club director
- space mechanic
- underwater archaeologist

Others that come to mind are:

- Chief Technology Officer (CTO)
- Chief Information Officer (CIO)
- Chief Knowledge Officer (CKO)
- Chief Geographic Officer (CGO)
- Chief Training Officer

- Chief Privacy Officer
- Cybrarian
- Portal Administrator

- Health Informatics Knowledge Worker
- e-Commerce
- Bioterrorism Specialist

In the United States the auto and related industries - steel, rubber, glass, aluminum, railroads and auto dealers - accounted for one-fifth of all employment in the United States in the 1980s. Today the employment in these fields decline as this type of work is automated and employment in service occupations increase.

Helpful Link

http://www.entrepreneur.com/

REFLECTION NOTES

REFLECTION NOTES

REFLECTION NOTES

Smarter Résumés: A Passion Driven Job Search

Chapter 2

INTERVIEWING

Chapter 2

INTERVIEWING FOR A JOB

Purpose of the Interview

The interview is a mutual exchange of information between an employer and a candidate for a position. The primary objectives are:

- To supply information about yourself that is not contained in your résumé; to show that you understand yourself and have a sense of direction in your career.

- To enable the employer to evaluate your personality and attitudes in terms of the demands of the organization and the possible position.

- To enable you to gain information about the organization and the job.

- To give you and the employer an opportunity to discuss the desirability of further contact or an offer of employment.

Knowledge of Yourself

To impress an employer you must be well prepared and understand the value of what you have to offer and be able to relate your assets to the position and the organization. To accomplish this you must know yourself, your strengths and weaknesses. Review your self assessment results and occupational information. Review your résumé and the job description. Be prepared to answer questions about the contents and substantiate all points with information. Employers may want to determine the level you are currently functioning and how you have grown over time in areas related to position, interpersonal and work skills, and motivation. Some will ask you to talk about your failures and mistakes to find out what you have learned or have since done differently.

Knowledge of Company/Organization

You must be familiar with the position and the organization so that you can demonstrate how and why you will be an effective employee. Try to find out as much as you can about the organization prior to your interview. Ask the company to send you material, such as the annual report, brochures, in-house newsletters or magazines. Review the organization's Web site. Obtain information, if you can, on whom you will be meeting with and the schedule for the interview period. If you can find out about your interviewer such as, their names, titles, and background, in advance, you will be able to commit their names to memory and use them during the interviews.

Dress For Success

Your success or failure in the interview can depend on your appearance and the interviewer's first impression of you. If it is not good, it will be much harder during the rest of the interview to change the interviewer's mind. Look neat, clean and well-groomed. Select proper clothing for the type of organization interviewing you. The generally accepted standard is to dress similar to the supervisors. If in doubt, be conservative.

Unless your job requires you to wear a uniform, choosing clothing for work can be difficult. Of course there are industry standards, such as the navy blue suit for accountants and bankers. What do you wear,  however, if you work in an industry where there really isn't a typical style of dress? Complicating the matter further are companies that allow more casual attire. How do you keep from crossing over the line from casual to sloppy? What about the job interview? You want to look your professional best, but you also want to appear as if you "fit in". Here are some pointers for dressing for any type of work situation:

- First and foremost, no matter what you wear, your clothes should be neat and clean.

MEN

- **Suit:** Professional slacks and a jacket

- *Note: Jacket should be buttoned when standing or walking. When wearing a jacket with three buttons, center button should be buttoned. When wearing a jacket with two buttons, top one should be buttoned*

- **Pressed Shirt:** Long-Sleeved white shirts test best in business settings. Always wear an undershirt, and never wear a short-sleeved shirt under a suit— even during summer.
- *Note: Shirt cuffs should extend 1/2 inch below jacket sleeve.*

- **Tie:** Choose an updated silk tie, keeping in mind the importance of width. (Less than three inches in width is considered in fashion)
- *Note: the tip of the tie should barely touch the top of your belt buckle. Also, the pattern should be small, subtle and repetitive.*

- **Dress Shoes:** Wear shoes to match your belt, but be sure to never wear casual shoes like hush puppies, penny loafers, or sneakers.

- *Leather Belt:* A black or burgundy belt to match your shoes should always be worn if your pants have belt loops.

- *Socks:* All socks should reach to your mid-calf. A "flash of skin" due to short socks is never professional.

- *Professional watch:* Never wear a watch with a plastic band; a metal or leather band is best.

- *Close shave or well-groomed facial hair.*

- *Cologne:* A small amount goes a long way.

- *Clean nails:* *Complete the grooming process by cleaning your nails.*

WOMEN

- *Professional skirt suit or pant-suit:* Navy, grey, taupe, and black are all conservative suit colors to invest in when building your career wardrobe.

- *Note:* mini-skirts may be in style, but *not* in the workplace. Calf-length skirts are always more appropriate.

- *Pressed blouse*
- *Closed-toe and closed-heel shoes:* The classic leather pump is ideal

Smarter Résumés: A Passion Driven Job Search

in black, navy, or taupe. Also, heels should measure approximately three inches in height.

- *Note:* Many individuals look at the condition of other people's shoes to determine whether they pay   attention to detail. Shoes should always be polished and clean.

- ***Hosiery:*** Stockings add a necessary finished look. Go with a skin-toned color or a dark color if your suit is the same dark color.

- *Note:* Be sure to take an extra pair of hosiery with you in case you accidentally run the pair you have on.

- ***Light Jewelry:*** Wear no more than one ring on each hand, and wear simple yet elegant earrings (preferably no dangling earrings).

- *Note:* Simplicity is the key. If you think you might be wearing too much jewelry, it is probably a good idea to eliminate a piece.

- ***Light Make-up:*** The goal is to look natural

- ***Neat, clean Hair:***
- Shoulder-length or shorter hair tests best in business. If your hair is longer than shoulder length, wear it pulled up or back in a style that will give you a chic look.
- *Note: Avoid girlish hair bows*

Interview Questions

For a list of sample interview questions and information relating to questions that are illegal for the employer to ask on an interview, go to

INTERVIEW QUESTIONS

Questions to Ask the Employer

Ask intelligent, well thought out questions to show the employer you are serious about the organization and need more information. The questions, however, should be pertinent to the position and reflect your enthusiasm and knowledge.

Examples:

- What do you see as the priorities for someone in this position?
- Would you be able to describe a typical day on the job?
- What would be a typical first-year assignment?
- What training programs do you have available for your employees?
- What level of responsibility could I expect in this position?
- What qualities do you look for in new employees?
- Is there a typical career path for a person in this position?
- How are employees evaluated and promoted?
- What is a realistic timeframe for promotion?
- Does the company have a promotion-from-within policy?

- What are the company's plans for the future?
- What do you see as the greatest threat to the organization?
- What/where are the greatest opportunities for the organization?
- How would you describe your organization's management style and working
- environment
- What do you like most about your organization?
- Why is this position available? (Is it a new job or where did the former employee go?)
- I feel confident that I would be able to do your job well, but do you have any doubts about my suitability?
- Do you have a copy of the detailed job description?

Verbal/Non-Verbal Communication

In the United States, acknowledge introductions with a smile and a firm handshake. Maintain good eye contact and smile when appropriate. Be enthusiastic and responsive. Radiate energy. How are you going to demonstrate your enthusiasm if you tend to be a quiet person? As you talk about your past and present activities in answer to questions, your passion and energy can be communicated both through the words of your stories and your body language (sparkling eyes and tone of voice).

Sit comfortably, without slouching. Don't put anything on your lap or in your hands as it will restrict your natural body movement and you may be tempted to "play" with it. Keep your clipboard, note pad, briefcase, or portfolio on the floor beside your chair for easy retrieval when necessary.

Respond to questions specifically and concisely but give sufficient details to enable the interviewer to evaluate your credentials. Interviewers become frustrated when they have to listen to long rambling answers. Think before you speak. It is quite acceptable to pause before talking in order to organize your thoughts, but think quietly. Avoid verbal fillers such as um, ah, you know, etc., or repeating the question in order to provide thinking time. Use business language. Avoid slang. Speak clearly.

Prepare in advance to talk about any topic that you are concerned or feel uncomfortable about. If there is something that you don't want an interviewer to inquire about, you can be sure that somehow the interviewer will sense it, and ask. Practice your answer out loud often enough to feel confident when saying it. Maintain poise and self control. Maybe you need to think about that difficult issue as a learning opportunity which has made you a better person. Answer questions truthfully. If you are playing a game in order to get hired, you will be found out once you are on the job.

Types of Interviews

One-On-One

The most common interview format is one interviewer speaking with one candidate.

Team/Board Interview with Two or More Persons

In the United States, the key is good eye-to-eye contact with the person who asks you the question, but remembers to look at the other persons present periodically in order to include them in your answer. Review the information relating to <u>personality types</u>. Because there will be various  personality types represented, it is important to realize they will be evaluating your responses from a variety of perspectives; some personality styles want details others the global perspective, some logic based others values based answers, some are looking for decision makers others want open to other ideas. Answer each question from more than one perspective, for example, give the big picture and supplement it with details; give a logical bottom line answer but supplement it with a values based comment.

Structured Interview

All candidates are asked the same questions for the employer's ease in evaluating applicants. If there is important information that you have not conveyed by the end of the interview, when asked if you have any questions or anything to add, present your additional qualifications. Usually the interviewer will make written notes of your answers.

Unstructured Interview

In an unstructured interview, you have a better opportunity to convey information as there is no set agenda for questions by the interviewer. However, you will have greater responsibility for structuring the interview, you need to be well prepared and know the points you want to make.

Telephone Interview

Because of the high cost of paying travel expenses for candidates to the employer's location, some first interviews are being conducted over the phone. If the call surprises you and you are

not ready for an interview, ask the person to call back in 15 minutes, or arrange another time which will be mutually convenient. You need time to refresh your memory on the organization and what points about yourself you want to make. All points about good interview skills still apply. You just do not have to dress for the occasion. However, you may find that dressing up may help you perform better. Keep your résumé and your list of questions to ask in front of you. Have a pen and paper available to note any comments or questions you may have during the interview.

Computer Interviews

Because of the number of qualified applicants available for positions, you may find that your first interview will be with a computer. The purpose of this  screening is to compare your answers to the information on your résumé. Be just as diligent with your answers as you would with a human interviewer. You don't want the computer to find reasons to screen you out.

Video Conferencing

Computer technology through on-line interview rooms allows companies to prescreen more candidates from farther afield than has

been possible through visits to colleges and universities in the past. The pool of applicants then invited to t he company for personal interviews can be more comprehensive. Recruiters conduct live, face-to-face interviews with job applicants via personal computers equipped with cameras and speakers. Use the same strategies you would if you were meeting in person... Clothing, body language, and dialogue do not differ. Your agenda is to be offered an invitation to meet personally for a second interview at the company.

Second Interview - Plant/Office Visit

Except for short-term positions, a candidate being seriously considered by a prospective employer will be invited to visit the organization at one of its locations. One purpose is to provide you with an opportunity to meet other staff. The second is to give more people an opportunity to interview you at greater depth to determine whether a good match is developing. The visit can take an entire day, sometimes more. When an organization offers to pay your expenses to travel to the interview, be prudent in submitting costs. Your choice of moderate rather than luxurious accommodation, food, transportation, etc. will reflect your good judgment.

Ending the Interview

When it appears that the interviewer is about to end the interview, there are certain points you should make sure you have covered before you leave the room:

- Be aware of the interview process yet to come before a candidate is selected for the job (another interview in same/other location, meetings with other individuals in the organization, etc.)

- Ask the interviewer when you can expect to hear about a decision or ask when you should make an inquiry as a follow-up.

- Express your interest in the position and thank the interviewer for interviewing you.

- Ask for a business card or ensure that you have the interviewer's name, title, address so that you can send a thank-you letter. Make sure your letter arrives within 24 hours of the interview.

Employer Evaluation

Employers usually have a formal rating sheet with predetermined areas such as:

- neat and clean overall appearance/poise/communicative skills
- academic/work achievements (learning ability, standards of excellence)

- special skills (technical, languages, creativity, management, analytic, negotiation)
- personal characteristics (team player, enthusiasm, dependability, emotional stability, flexibility)
- assessment, goals/ambitions
- leisure-time activities, balance in life
- reaction to job/organization
- potential

Evaluating Your Performance

To evaluate how well you did after each interview, ask yourself:

- What points did I make that seemed to interest the employer?
- Did I present my qualifications in the best manner possible, giving appropriate examples as evidence?
- Did I pass up opportunities to sell myself, to demonstrate the work I do, and to show how profitably I could do it for both the organization and myself?
- Did I talk too much? Too little?
- Was I too tense? Passive? Aggressive?
- Did I find out enough about the employer and the job to help in making a knowledgeable decision?

Write down some changes you would like to make in your next interview.

Evaluating Your Job Offer

When you receive a job offer it is important to review the opportunity in light of your long term goals, findings in your assessment results, occupational exploration, and company research to help you understand if this is offer is a match.

Employer Contact Record

Keep a record of your employer research information and contact information.

Employer Research	Organization
Name of the organization	Address, Phone
Type of industry	Initial Contact Date
Products and services	Employer Response Date
Financial picture	My Follow-up Date
Size of company	Job Interview Notes
Contact Information	Job Offer Date
Person, Title	

Informational Interview and Job Shadowing

One of the best sources for gathering information about what's happening in an occupation or an industry is to talk to people working in the field. This process is called informational or research interviewing. An informational interview is an interview that you initiate - you ask the questions. The purpose is to obtain information, not to get a job.

One of the most effective methods of obtaining more detailed information about a particular career is to conduct an information interview with someone who holds the position that interests you. The benefits are numerous:

- To build confidence for your job interviews
- To expand your professional network
- To explore careers and clarify your career goal
- Allows you to determine whether the career, industry or company matches your skills, interests and expectations
- To identify your professional strengths and weaknesses
- Confirms information that you have read and provides information not available in written form assists you in organizing your future job search by revealing the best ways to get into the profession
- Provides you with tips and information about the job and career field that could be of great value in preparing applications for work and in a job interview
- To access the most up-to-date career information
- Gives you an opportunity to see the organization from the inside.

Preparation

Prepare for information interviews well in advance. You must begin with a self assessment. The better you know yourself the more likely you will pursue a career that is both enjoyable and rewarding.

Next, conduct a thorough search for information about the careers that interest you and on any organization you intend to contact. There are several sources that could provide the names and addresses of people with whom you might set up an information interview. Begin by checking the resources. If you are college graduate or enrolled in college, check with the Career Center.

The following are additional suggestions:

- Alumni Directory
- Employer Directories
- Yellow Pages
- Government, Ministries, and Departments
- Volunteer Directory

- Professional Associations
- Journals
- Internet
- Professors
- Family
- Friends

Contact the organization that interests you. Ask for the name, job title and phone number of the person doing the job you wish to investigate.

How to Arrange the Interview

Telephone or write the person you wish to interview well before the date the interview would take place. Introduce yourself and explain who you are (e.g., a student, a person thinking of changing jobs). Perhaps, mention how you found the person's name. State the type of work you are interested in researching, the reason why, and the amount of time it would take to conduct the interview (usually 20 - 30 minutes). If the person is unable to meet with you, ask for a referral.

Thank the person for speaking with you and confirm the date, time and location of the interview. If that person cannot see you, express your regret. State your appreciation for any referral names given to you.

The contact information for the person to be interviewed is:

Name:

Title:

Organization:

Address:

Phone Number:

The arrangements for the Information Interview as follows:

Date and Time of Interview:

Address where Interview will take place:

Parking Arrangements:

Time to Travel from Parking to Interview Location:

Other Information:

Conducting the Interview

You requested the interview. Be prepared to ask questions. Be concise so as not to waste the person's time. Allow the person an opportunity to provide additional information. Use a paper or electronic diary to keep track of your contacts and to add notes during your meetings. (You can continue to use the same log when you network.) If you have not already seen the work area, ask for a tour.

The purpose of the interview is to collect information that will allow you to make informed career decisions. Do not use the information interview to ask for a job or set up an employment interview.

Potential interview questions

Technically, not every item is a question; some are statements; but all are intended to prompt you for a response. Better questions are not those that can be answered with a "yes" or "no," but are open-ended questions that invite thoughtful response. Even if you are asked a question that can be answered with a "yes" or "no," (e.g. "Are you comfortable with the amount of travel this job involves?"), you can certainly add a word of explanation to back up your answer (e.g., "Yes. I actually look forward to the opportunity to travel and to work with the staff members in some of the other offices.)

Best questions are those that ask you how you behaved in the past, because past behavior is the best predictor of future behavior. These are referred to as behavioral interview questions.

Here is one list of sample behavioral-based interview questions:

- Describe a situation in which you were able to use persuasion to successfully convince someone to see things your way.
- Describe a time when you were faced with a stressful situation that demonstrated your coping skills.
- Give me a specific example of a time when you used good judgment and logic in solving a problem.
- Give me an example of a time when you set a goal and were able to meet or achieve it.
- Tell me about a time when you had to use your presentation skills to influence someone's opinion.
- Give me a specific example of a time when you had to conform to a policy with which you did not agree.
- Please discuss an important written document you were required to complete.

- Tell me about a time when you had to go above and beyond the call of duty in order to get a job done.
- Tell me about a time when you had too many things to do and you were required to prioritize your tasks.
- Give me an example of a time when you had to make a split second decision.
- What is your typical way of dealing with conflict? Give me an example.
- Tell me about a time you were able to successfully deal with another person even when that individual may not have personally liked you (or vice versa).
- Tell me about a difficult decision you've made in the last year.
- Give me an example of a time when something you tried to accomplish and failed.
- Give me an example of when you showed initiative and took the lead.
- Tell me about a recent situation in which you had to deal with a very upset customer or co-worker.
- Give me an example of a time when you motivated others.
- Tell me about a time when you delegated a project effectively.
- Give me an example of a time when you used your fact-finding skills to solve a problem.
- Tell me about a time when you missed an obvious solution to a problem.

- Describe a time when you anticipated potential problems and developed preventive measures.
- Tell me about a time when you were forced to make an unpopular decision.
- Please tell me about a time you had to fire a friend.
- Describe a time when you set your sights too high (or too low).

Not every interviewer will ask you every one of these questions. However, if you are prepared to address these questions, you will leave the impression that you were prepared for your job interview, even if additional questions take you by surprise.

• What are your long-range goals and objectives for the next seven to ten years?

• What are your short-range goals and objectives for the next one to three years?

• How do you plan to achieve your career goals?

• What are the most important rewards you expect in your career?

• Why did you choose the career for which you are preparing?

• What are your strengths, weaknesses, and interests?

• How do you think a friend or professor who knows you well would describe you?

• Describe a situation in which you had to work with a difficult person (another student, co-worker, customer, supervisor, etc.). How did you handle the situation? Is there anything you would have done differently in hindsight?

• What motivates you to put forth your greatest effort? Describe a situation in which you did so.

• In what ways have your college experiences prepared you for a career?

• How do you determine or evaluate success?

• In what ways do you think you can make a contribution to our organization?

• Describe a contribution you have made to a project on which you worked.

• What qualities should a successful manager/leader/supervisor/etc. possess?

• Was there an occasion when you disagreed with a supervisor's decision or company policy?

• Describe how you handled the situation.

• What two or three accomplishments have given you the most satisfaction? Why?

• Describe your most rewarding college experience.

• What interests you about our product or service?

• Why did you select your college or university?

- What led you to choose your major or field of study?
- What college subjects did you like best? Why?
- What college subjects did you like least? Why?
- If you could do so, how would you plan your academic studies differently?
- Do you think your grades are a good indication of your academic achievement?
- What have you learned from participation in extracurricular activities?
- In what kind of work environment are you most comfortable?
- How do you work under pressure?
- Describe a situation in which you worked as part of a team. What role did you take on? What went well and what didn't?
- In what part-time, co-op, or summer jobs have you been most interested? Why?
- How would you describe the ideal job for you following graduation?
- Why did you decide to seek a position with our organization?
- What two or three things would be most important to you in your job?
- What criteria are you using to evaluate the organization for which you hope to work?
- How would you view needing to relocate for the job? Do you have any constraints on relocation?

• Are you comfortable with the amount of travel this job requires?

• Are you willing to spend at least six months as a trainee?

What the interview is looking for:

Interviewer says: Tell me about yourself.

Remember, this is a job interview, not a psychological or personal interview. The interviewer is interested in the information about you that relates to your qualifications for employment, such as education, work experiences and extracurricular activities.

Interviewer says: What do you expect to be doing five years from now? Ten years from now?

The interviewer is looking for evidence of career goals and ambitions rather than minutely specific descriptions. The interviewer wants to see your thought process and the criteria that are important to you. The interviewer is not looking for information about your personal life.

Interviewer says: Why should I hire you?

Stress what you have to offer the employer as relates to the position for which you are interviewing, not how nice it would be to work there or what you want from the employer. Remember that you are being compared to other candidates, and in fact more than one candidate might be a very good employee. Deliver to the employer reasons to see that you are a good fit (show you know yourself, know the field/industry, know the organization, and know the position).

Interviewer says: What are your ideas about salary?
Research salaries in your field before your interviews so that you know the current salary range for the type of position you are seeking. Read more about being prepared for questions about salary.

Interviewer says: Why do you want to work for our company/organization?
Not having an answer is a good way to get crossed off the candidate list, and is a common pet peeve of interviewers. Research the employer before your interview; attempt to find out about the organization's products, locations, clients, philosophy, goals, previous growth record and growth plans, how they value employees and customers, etc.

Unfortunately it's very common for job-seekers to directly state, "I really want to work for your company/agency/organization/firm," but then to be unable to answer the question "why?" Without the answer to "why?" the initial statement becomes meaningless.

Smarter Résumés: A Passion Driven Job Search

Salary Research Links

Salary.com

PayScale.com

Glassdoor.com

After the Interview

- Add more information to the notes you took during the interview.

- Always send a thank you letter promptly (within 1-2 days after the interview).

- Summarize what was learned during the Information Interview.

REFLECTION NOTES

Smarter Résumés: A Passion Driven Job Search

REFLECTION NOTES

REFLECTION NOTES

REFLECTION NOTES

Chapter 3

RÉSUMÉ BUILDING

Chapter 3

RÉSUMÉ BUILDING

The résumé is a marketing tool which acts as a door opener and allows an employer to assess your qualifications quickly in the prescreening process before interviews. A résumé is a concise illustration of your past experience, which grabs attention and gets you an interview. It is a critical marketing tool in your personal  marketing campaign - which is what the job search process really is. Your résumé should be succinct, commanding and truthful. It should emphasize skills, strengths and accomplishments. Most résumés are initially read for 15 seconds or less (3-5 seconds if unsolicited). Help the readers form mental pictures of you and your activities as the look for key words and phrases. The employer needs to ascertain the benefits you are offering based on your past accomplishments.

The résumé is a more concise presentation of credentials than a curriculum vitae which is prepared for a teaching/research position in a university or for inclusion in an application package for graduate school. There are 3 kinds of résumés: electronic version, paper version for scanning, and standardized form which requires you to fill in the blanks from which an employer or company matches résumés to jobs.

As part of the research you do on an organization, you may want to determine if you need to submit a résumé for scanning.

- Supply a good laser quality document, on 8½ x 11, white or very light-colored paper; use a sans serif font such as Arial, with point size 10 or larger; avoid embellishments such as parentheses, brackets, horizontal lines.

- As mentioned in #3 above, italics, bolding, etc. may also prove problematic in some instances.

- If using a very basic formatting program, ensure that your headings are clearly seen by being featured at the left margin. By indenting your text under your heading, you will be able to show visually what belongs together.

Additional Tips

- Employers looking at your résumé want to easily find the keywords relating to their needs. Also, when your résumé is stored in a database, an employer will use the computer to conduct a keyword search. Your résumé will not be selected unless you have a "hit" with the minimum number of keywords requested. Your résumé will not be near the top of the list unless you have all or most of the keywords they used.

- Interactive multimedia résumés are becoming more common with the advances in both hardware and software. If you choose this type, remember that some employers may not have the latest equipment to download your résumé with sound and complex graphics quickly, or at all. But you could try; you may get noticed over other applicants.
- Always have a subject in your subject line when sending an e-mail résumé to an employer. A precise reference to their job and your fit may spark their desire to read your résumé rather than to hit the delete key.
- Include information on technology skills.

One student suggested a nice way to communicate that you plan to transfer to a four year school. I enhanced it to be more specific. Below is an example:

EDUCATION:

A. A. Liberal Arts Santiago Canyon College In Progress
Transfer Program to:
B. A. Business Administration Specialization in Restaurant Management
The Collings School of Hospitality Management at California State Poly Pomona

Focus

It is important to tailor your qualifications to the job for which you are applying. To do this, review your assessment results, the description of the job you have found in your occupational exploration, and the job description provided by the employer. Look for information provided by professional organizations to determine trends in the field. Before starting a draft of your résumé, summarize your points a worksheet. Include the following information.

Job Title or Type of Work

(Focus your strengths and related examples to this target market. Prepare additional sheets for other jobs)

Job Description Summary

- Rate your oral and written communication skills (e.g., excellent, good, etc.). Include your ability to listen. Give examples of when you demonstrated those skills.
- Rate your interpersonal skills. Give an example.
- Rate your ability to plan and organize. Give an example.
- Describe a situation where you had to solve a problem. What was the outcome? What does this tell an employer about your critical thinking/analytical/problem solving capabilities?

- Everyone is creative. Discuss aspects of your creativity (e.g., generating ideas, design, etc.).
- Would you consider yourself flexible or adaptable? How would you convince an employer?
- Give a good example of your initiative or self motivation.
- Give a good example of your teamwork.
- Give a good example of your leadership.
- Give a good example of your time management skills.
- Did you ever do more than was required of you by your job description or supervisor? Describe.
- The world continues to change at a rapid pace. Perhaps even faster in the future than in the past. Do you see yourself as having a positive role in this change? If so, how can you help an employer?
- Discuss your computer knowledge and experience.
- List your achievements which form a good basis for the job.
- Discuss your level of comfort with the risk taking required.
- Add your other strengths as required by the job.

In summary, when an employer asks you, "Why do you want to work for us?", what would you say to show your interest in and knowledge of the organization based on your research? When an employer asks you, "Why should I hire you?", what would you say to convince the interviewer you are the best person for the job? Organize your major strengths in the following areas and give examples or illustrations as proof, including a statement on the success you achieved.

- Work content or technical knowledge or skills (e.g., forecasting). Name skill, and give an example of a time you demonstrated this strength.
- Transferable skills to almost any job (team player). Name skill, and give an example of where that experience could benefit the prospective new employer.
- Personality or self management skills (attention to detail). Name skill, and give an example of a situation where this strength proved valuable.

Résumé Style and Appearance

The first impression of your résumé should be favorable for both your electronic and paper versions: well organized material, easy-to-read font, correct grammar and spelling, up-to-date information. Your paper copies should be printed on good quality paper and have no handwritten corrections or white out.

One to two pages of information should be sufficient to present your credentials clearly and concisely for the position. Only in rare cases would you need to go to three pages, but then all three pages must contain essential information needed by an employer to judge your qualifications. You may get only one chance for that interview. Write in point form and double check that all pertinent key words are there. You want to make it easy for both a human reader and the computer to find the information they are looking for.

Prepare a completely positive document to present your skills. Don't be shy! However, the résumé must be an honest evaluation. Don't lie. The misrepresentation will come back to haunt you, if not in the interview, then on the job.

There is no one right résumé. Create a document that sells your strengths. Since employers are looking for the best value for their hiring dollar, you should market what makes you different from your classmates or anyone else wanting an interview for that job.

Many of your strengths are revealed through both your content and style of writing, e.g., enthusiasm, confidence, reliability, communication skills.

Multimedia Portfolio

Online multimedia portfolios are becoming more popular. Components may include: cover letter, objective, experience, education, transferable skills, technical skills, language fluencies, awards, community activities, and references in multimedia format; a printable copy of the résumé may also be included. Portfolios can also showcase projects such as an art gallery and written reports and it demonstrates computer literacy on the part of the presenter.

An electronic version of your résumé is somewhat different from those prepared on paper. Some points:

- An employer can view the document one screen at a time, rather than glancing at the one or two pages to get a sense of your qualifications. Try to limit your information to five or six screens, with the first being the attention grabber.

- Name and Summary of Qualifications in point form are at the top of the first screen. You may also be able to get your name, address, phone, fax, e-mail at the bottom of the first screen. If not, that information will be at the top of the second screen, to be followed by your Job Objective. The order of your other headings can be similar to those on your paper résumé. Keep the information in each section targeted to the job you want, leave off old or unrelated jobs and activities.
- You don't want to get a message from an employer saying that your résumé was unreadable. You may want to check with the computer databases you are considering listing your résumé with, or the recent software and books, for more information about formatting. ASCII (text only) and HTML are currently being used. In some instances, the usual formatting techniques to create interest and readability, such as italicizing, bolding, underlining, may make your words illegible as some computer equipment cannot process those features. Bullets before points sometimes also cause problems. There may be several options you can choose from, some creating very attractive résumés which can be sent through e-mail.

A sample of an online multimedia portfolio can be found at:
http://sacacc.sac.edu/pres/résumé/JohnDoe2002/start.htm

A multimedia portfolio is a showcase of your talents or past work that uses more than one medium to communicate. A traditional résumé uses only the medium of text to communicate your work history, while a traditional portfolio uses images with only minimal text. A multimedia portfolio can combine text, audio, video and still images to give an m ore comprehensive presentation of your past work.

Who Uses Multimedia Portfolios

People in creative professions have used multimedia portfolios to showcase visual artworks, films and music for decades. However, with multimedia software readily available for home computers, other professionals also can take advantage of multimedia portfolios. For example, a real estate professional can put together a video of still photos showing recent home sales and satisfied customers, mixed with text that highlights his strengths and focus as a real estate agent. Underscoring this portfolio with music can help clients who view the portfolio become immersed in the mood the agent wants them to experience.

Benefits

A multimedia portfolio gives prospective employers or clients a more comprehensive view of your experience than a text or image-only portfolio might. Audio-visual information is often easier for the client or employers to comprehend due to the benefit of visual cues and body language, which can help others get a better idea of who you are, if you place footage of yourself in the video or images. Creating such a portfolio yourself also proves that you have computing skills that may be valuable to potential employers.

What to Include

Multimedia portfolios should be brief and only items that communicate an idea clearly and immediately should be included. For example, if you are a teacher creating a multimedia portfolio of your work, you can include video clips of classroom projects, as well as stills of their finished work and text with your résumé highlights. When choosing the video clips, settle on one idea to communicate per clip, such as your problem-solving skills or how you engage students in their work, and then cut that video down to the minimum amount of footage required to get the idea across. Create a version of the portfolio that is less than two minutes long as a quick highlight. Also create a longer version if you feel more is necessary to document your work.

Preparing for a Multimedia Portfolio

The key to creating your own multimedia portfolio is to document your work as you are doing it. Whether you use photos, videos or your own art, keep visual and written records of what you do. When you are ready to put your portfolio together, find software that allows you to do this easily on your computer. Windows Movie Maker is free for Windows PC users, or you can use a program like PowerPoint or other software to create your portfolio.

Caution

If other people appear in your multimedia portfolio, you may need to have release forms to show that portfolio to others. This is especially true if you work with children and plan to showcase your portfolio online. Keep a stack of photo or video release forms with you when you document your work. Have people sign them to state that they consent to letting you use their images for portfolio purposes. You can create your own release forms or use standard forms; they are available online or at some office supply stores.

REFLECTION NOTES

Smarter Résumés: A Passion Driven Job Search

REFLECTION NOTES

REFLECTION NOTES

REFLECTION NOTES

Chapter 4
MAJOR SECTIONS
OF THE RÉSUMÉ

Chapter 4

MAJOR SECTIONS OF THE RÉSUMÉ

There are two basic components to a résumé. The first one is CONTENT (what the résumé is about). The second one is DESIGN (how the résumé looks). Both elements are critical in determining the success of your résumé. As you might guess, content is of greater value to the prospective employer. Content tells the employer about your qualifications,  such as your accomplishments, where you have worked before, how long you have worked at each job and so on.

The design element is quite a bit different, but it also plays a part in determining how well a résumé is written. Some of the areas that design entails are:

- color and quality of paper (white and 24 lb paper, at least)
- format (Chronological, Functional, Combination)
- layout (which sections appear first on the page)
- font(s) used (one or two at the most)
- white space (gives the reader's eyes a break)

Determining the design your résumé can contribute a **great deal** to the overall presentation you make to prospective employers. A résumé must not only contain the right language and qualifications, but it must be pleasing to the eye.

Look at it this way: When résumés are first taken out of their envelopes, the process of making a first impression begins. You can't take a chance of being ruled out, especially this early, so your materials must be of the highest quality.

Do you know what your competitors are doing? If not, then you need to ensure you are doing **everything possible** to give yourself an advantage over them. Keep in mind that they could just as easily be reading the same information you are right now. How are you going to out-perform them?

The next component of the résumé that you must strive to make PERFECT is the content portion. There is nothing of higher value than speaking to a prospective employer's needs. When you are able to communicate your achievements and abilities in such a way as to garner instant attention, then you have a good chance of getting a call for an interview.

That means you must tailor the content to each employer's specific needs for the position you are seeking. Using the same résumé for different employers is not the way you market yourself in today's competitive labor market. Each résumé must speak to a unique position at one company. A prospective employer can tell right away if a candidate has taken the time to focus his/her résumé in this way. It makes a tremendous difference in the way your résumé is handled (read vs. not read).

A hiring manager will know immediately if your résumé is being mass marketed to dozens of organizations. Each company has a language all its own. If you are not making an effort to speak the language of each company you send your résumé to, you will not find success in the job search process. It simply will not happen.

Your résumé **has to get the reader's attention** and the best way to do that is to inject the language of the prospective employer into the content wherever possible.

How do you do that?

You found out about the job, right? Was it from a newspaper ad? Did someone tell you about it? Research the organization to find out what matters to them. Ask questions of existing employees (in person or via phone). Yes, you can call Human Resources and request some general information about the company and even some specific information about the position they are attempting to fill. Check out their web presence.

The more you find out, the better you can tailor your résumé and cover letter to match their standards. Each organization has a culture (environment) that differs from others in a variety of ways. When

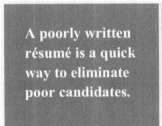

A poorly written résumé is a quick way to eliminate poor candidates.

you are able to clearly speak to the needs of the employer, **you will win immediate favor**. You will "belong" in a way that your competitors cannot.

Content is the most important aspect of the résumé since that is what employers will base their initial decisions on. Would you prefer to have your résumé set aside in the "yes" pile or the "no" pile? That is a dumb question, indeed. So, make the effort to ensure each section of your résumé is a work of art. Each résumé component is an essential element of the whole package that you present to a prospective employer. Each résumé component deserves the time and effort necessary to ensure your success in the job search process. Beat out your competitors by having the best résumé of anyone in your chosen career field.

Beginner Résumé Tips

If this is your first time writing a résumé, you will definitely benefit from some beginner résumé tips. Writing a résumé is not difficult, but it does take some time. Keep in mind, the more time you invest in creating your résumé, the better it will look and the better your chances will be for getting called for a job interview.

Some beginner résumé tips that are especially important for your first résumé are:

- Keep it focused – don't try to do anything other than let the employer know that you are capable of doing the job and doing it well. Include in your résumé anything that you have done in the past that relates to the position for which you are applying. For instance, if you are attempting to secure a position as an marketing assistant, then any education or work experience that shows you are able to perform the duties of an marketing assistant will improve your chances of being invited to an interview.

- Keep it short – since you are writing your first résumé, you probably will not have a great deal of information to include on your résumé, but don't worry, this is fine. Employers do understand that everyone has to start somewhere. Just be sure you use the résumé keywords that make employers sit up and take notice – as well as using the terms that are specific to your field – and you will make a good impression.

- Keep it real – never should you lie on your résumé. If you pad your résumé by including untruths and embellishing your experience, you will be found out sometime. It may be in the interview or it may be on the job – but someone will realize that you didn't tell the truth. That can lead to your getting fired or worse, especially if you lie on a federal document.

A résumé is so vital to the job search process. It helps you offer the prospective employer a "sneak peek" at you - your qualifications. If there were an easier way to bring employers and employees together, it would be wonderful, but at this time, the résumé (and cover letter) are what people use to present themselves to their future employers.

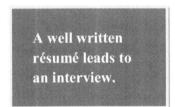

A well written résumé leads to an interview.

Even though it is not a lot of fun, spend whatever time it takes to make sure your résumé is as professionally written as possible. A good résumé is easy to spot and hiring managers are always on the lookout for qualified people. When you make a hiring manager's job easy by providing the right information in a clear, concise format, you will reap the rewards.

These Résumé Do's and Don'ts have been provided to ensure you are creating the best résumé possible. When you think about getting a job, the first thing that comes to mind is: "How do I get the employer's attention?" In today's competitive job market, the answer is: "You need a résumé." The short description is that it is a means for you to present yourself to a prospective employer. It is a piece of paper that details your personal background in such as way as to generate enough interest in the mind of the employer so that you are asked to meet face to face.

An employer does not have time to meet with every person who wants to work for them. Many times, hundreds of résumés can be sent in for a single job opening. No one has time to meet with hundreds of job candidates to determine if they are right for the job or not. A résumé gives the employer a way to evaluate an individual prior to a face to face meeting (job interview).

When an employer receives a stack of résumés, there is usually a quick scan of each résumé to determine if it should be read fully. This is often referred to as the "20 second scan" or the "30 second scans". Very little time is actually spent reading the résumé during this first stage. What the employer is first looking for is anything to weed out a candidate from the rest of the stack.

A résumé (poorly written) is a quick way to eliminate poor candidates. This is the main reason that a résumé has to be so well-written. Any typos or grammar errors could be the cause for elimination – even if the job candidate is otherwise outstanding.

If the goal of a résumé is to obtain an interview, then the résumé has to lead the employer to that goal. The best way to do that is to make sure it is accurate, contains no typos or grammar errors and highlights the job candidate's skills and accomplishments as amazingly as possible.

Writing a great résumé is a bit time consuming and requires patience and determination, but when it is done well, a job opportunity can quickly become a job offer.

Why is the résumé SO important?

It is important because the employer has no idea who you are. It represents you. You can't be there to speak for yourself, so your résumé has to do that in a clear and arousing way. Arousing? You want to arouse the employer's interest to the point that he/she makes a phone call to interview you. It gives you an opportunity to meet the employer face to face. That's why it has to be a professional piece of work. It's not that writing a résumé is hard. It isn't hard at all. When you have the right information, such as what is available on this site, you can present your own personal information in a way that makes you person of interest to employers.

It just takes a little time. A résumé can either get your foot in the door or get a door closed in your face. Write the best one you can and you'll likely find yourself with your foot in several doors.

Using a Personal Logo on a Résumé

A new trend is developing a personal logo to go in the header next to your name. For example, a person may create their own logo using their initials and place it in the top right corner of page. This extra touch can add style and personality to your application. Think about what your personal logo means before you place it on the top of your résumé though. It should not just be there for  the sake of style, but if it better represents your personality, then it can be a fun way for your employer to get to know you and remember you. This way you can easily brand yourself, using that logo on all your social media and networking sites.

If you choose to use graphics and logos in your résumé though, then be aware of the hazards. Use it wisely and strategically so that your résumé better markets your skills. Don't add pictures just for the sake of it. Too much of them will make your résumé look sloppy and childish. You should be aware of your audience as well. Perhaps one employer would appreciate graphics, while another would not. Try to target your résumé to the audience, which may require you to have several résumés that are formatted differently. Finally, adding too many graphics will increase your file size. They also may not translate correctly when sent electronically. An oversized file will take longer to open, so an employer may disregard your application based on the extra time or effort it takes to open. But in general, a tasteful choice of graphics can add the final touch to your application.

Formatting Your Résumé

The format of your résumé depends on the job you are applying for as well as the phase in your career path. For example, if you are in college or a newly graduate, then place your educational information first. If you have more impressive work experience than educational experience, then place your work experience towards the top. Always list experience in reverse chronological order. This way your most recent, and therefore relevant information will appear first.

There are three main types of résumé formats. The first and most common is the Chronological résumé, which lists work history in reverse chronological order. However, this is not always the best format for all job seekers. The hiring manager will see clearly where you have worked in the past and whether or not you have worked in the same type of position, which could be a disservice.

If your past experience is not a perfect fit for the position you are currently applying for, then the Functional résumé is a second option. This structures the list by accomplishments under headers like "Sales" or "Management." If you have long gaps in employment, then this format may be a better option as well so that it focuses on your accomplishments rather than your

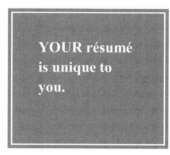

YOUR résumé is unique to you.

time off. Unfortunately, experienced recruiters know that the Functional résumé is generally used to hide a lack of qualifications, so they may not be fooled by the format.

The final option is the Hybrid résumé. This is a combination of the other two formats. It starts with a strong introduction that lists your qualifications and skills. After this introduction, list your work history with descriptions that show your accomplishments on the job.

Before you send out your résumé though, take a look over it. You may need to change or emphasize certain parts of your résumé depending on the job you apply for. Customize your résumé to reflect the most important qualifications that you have for this particular position.

Save a space for a concise list of skills that you have required. For example, list computer skills, language skills, and similar assets that could help you in the position. You do not need to include a list of references in your résumé. A résumé should not exceed a single page, so don't add unnecessary information. Instead, keep a separate list of references that you can provide if the employer asks for it.

Job seekers sometimes think that it is better to make their résumé stand out with unorthodox formats. It is better to create a résumé that is easy to read and understand because your plan may backfire and an employer may not invest the extra seconds it takes to figure out a strange format. Use standard texts like Times New Roman, Arial, and Verdana. Use MS-Word alignment and spacing rather than tabs. This standard formatting prevents the document from being improperly converted on different computers. Use MS-Word bullets as well instead of graphics or logos so that the format stays standard. Any kind of graphics or images on your résumé may cause formatting problems when it is converted to HTML, so double check these logos before sending the résumé.

Your résumé is unique to you. It relates your professional history in an enticing way that employers must find irresistible. You have to make your qualifications sound so awesome that the employer will not WANT to call anyone else. You will be a *perfect* match for the employer and the vacant position.

Write a Résumé that Works!

Yes, that seems like an obvious comment, but not everyone follows that advice.

For instance, many people put their résumés together without a lot of thought or attention to detail. Employers know right away who took a lot of time to make their résumé *shine* and who didn't. If you are willing to take the time to do this process right, you'll achieve far more success, get faster results and make more money. Sounds like a no-brainer, right?

NOTE: The successful use of an objective statement targets each position the candidate is seeking. No two jobs are exactly alike. No two objective statements should truly ever be the same, either.

Your objective statement should be very narrowly focused on each position. Use the knowledge you have about the position, the company (even the person reading your résumé if you know who it is) to write the most effective objective statement possible.

At some point down the road, you may want to use more than one variation of your résumé. For example, if you have worked in the field of Public Relations, you may want one copy that is directed toward a Public Relations position. Another copy might be geared toward a Marketing position (and so on). Some people have as many as 5 varieties depending upon their work experience and career goals. This can be very helpful during the job-search process.

It takes time.

Writing a history of your professional life takes time. There is a huge payoff if you do it yourself, though. Many job-seekers don't consider this aspect of writing a résumé, but **I'll tell you the secret**. When you take the time to write your own résumé, you know the material forward and backward and can recite it promptly and thoroughly when asked about it in an interview. This is SO important. It cannot be overstated.

You won't be fumbling for dates or job descriptions like some people do when they have a commercial service create their résumé for them. You'll know it all because you will have worked with the material in a variety of ways. **You gain so much more by doing the work yourself.** This, of course, is aside from the fact that you'll be saving a lot of money, too.

NAME AND CONTACT INFORMATION

Include name, address(es), telephone numbers, (voice/fax), e-mail, URL. No other personal information is required.

If you will be leaving a local address while your résumé is in circulation, note when (e.g., until April 20, 20xx). If you will not be personally answering your phone during business hours, list a number and/or e-mail address where an employer can leave a message for you. Decide what headings you will use if you need to state two addresses, e.g., one "local" or "present" and the other perhaps "home" or "permanent" if applying in that community or "alternate" for applications further afield. If you include the URL for your web pages, make sure the pages are in professional, business-like condition. Your site can include your résumé, examples of your work, e.g., code, drawings, etc.

If you are a foreign student you may have access to other opportunities to work in the United States on a temporary basis after graduation. Check with the Immigration Office. Decide whether you would like to include a notation about short-term employment on your résumé, e.g., Available {month/day/year} for one year contract. If you do not include this information on your résumé, definitely discuss it in your interview.

THE OBJECTIVE SECTION

The objective section is an essential part of your résumé. It tells the potential employer what you are looking for. It is not a place to boldly sell yourself. It is, rather, a place to state what you can offer the employer. Used correctly, it can help you get the job you WANT.

There is a way to incorporate a "selling" aspect into this section of the résumé without being obvious. You'll learn this little secret so that you can *impress the employer before you ever meet face-to-face.* Here is a good example of a job objective. This example is for a human resources management position.

Job Target: A challenging management or generalist position in Human Resources where my in-depth knowledge of HRIS systems can broaden the base of expertise in your department

Why is this example good?

It offers a great deal of information about the job candidate immediately. The candidate knows the language of Human Resources, wants to make valuable contributions to the organization, likes to be challenged, is flexible (will look at more than one position), communicates well and has experience in vital areas.

Good Résumé Objectives

Résumés are an excellent and professional way to exhibit an individual's accomplishments and skills. Résumés are directed towards potential employers, and often capitalize on your previous relevant experiences and at the same time exploiting your potential positives that you can bring to the company. Résumé objectives are simple yet crucially important phrases that are extremely specific to showcase your skills and desires to work for this potential employer. Résumé objectives are generally directly specified to the specific company of which you are applying.

Such as:

- Obtain a position at ABC Company where I can maximize my skills as a potential manager/ quality insurance manager/ program development.

  Explaining to your potential employer the importance of this job, and the earnest hard work you as an individual will do while working for the company is always a plus:

- To obtain a position that will enable me to use my strong organizational skills, educational background, and ability to work well with people.

Résumé objectives are a way to seem more personable and explain directly why you are a well fit candidate for the position. Furthermore, résumé objectives are a tool that should be utilized to increase the likelihood of you being hired.

The more obvious advertisement of your abilities and education comes later in the résumé (and also in the cover letter).

Consider for a moment just what this portion of the résumé is designed to do:

- Clarify for the employer what type of position you are seeking

- Define some of your finest qualities and present them in vibrant language to which the employer can immediately relate

- Subtly build up the employer with a positive flow of words

For co-op, summer, internship, part-time jobs: a job objective is not essential but highly recommended to give the employer an idea of what you want to do. For on-going (permanent) or contract jobs: a focused statement is essential. "Career Goal" tends to refer to a desired position that has a longer term association, while "Job Objective" can refer to an interim or more temporary type of job, e.g., Forensic Chemist for a career goal and Laboratory Technician for a job objective. State your goal or objective in terms of what you can do for an employer, not what you want an employer to do for you. Avoid expressions such as "...where I can use my knowledge and skills to expand my expertise in...". Phrase statement in terms of the job you want now, by job title (e.g., Computer Programmer, Social Worker, Technical Writer) or area (e.g., Communications, Public Relations, Health Education). Prepare two or more résumés to tailor qualifications if you are seeking different types of jobs.

SUMMARY OF QUALIFICATIONS

This section will provide a concise overview of your qualifications as they relate to your Job Objective or Career Goal as stated immediately above. Here is where you want the employer to recognize and become interested in the competitive advantage you bring to the position. Therefore, avoid a historical record.

State the value you are offering. Include the key words that would be used in a computer search of a database. This is the most difficult section of your résumé to write. Do not attempt it until the rest of your résumé is completely written because you need to see and understand the information before you can summarize it. Include three to seven points, using nouns and adjectives, not action verbs. Draw upon your work experience, volunteer and/or extracurricular activities in terms of duration, scope, accomplishments, etc. If you lack relevant experience, emphasize those skills you have developed in terms of interpersonal, organizational, supervisory, etc.

- First statement summarizes the experience you have related to your job objective, e.g., one year experience in graphic design.
- Second statement describes your working knowledge of the various components or aspects of the position (e.g., budgeting, report writing, program planning).
- Third statement outlines the various skills you possess to do the work effectively (e.g., problem solving, communication, time management).
- Fourth statement may refer to any academic background you have that complements your practical experience (e.g., machine design, resource assessment, and marketing).
- Fifth statement lists your personal characteristics and attitudes as required on the job (e.g., reliable, able to work under pressure, creative).

SKILLS SUMMARY (in place of Job Objective and Summary of Qualifications sections)

This section is essential for résumés without a Job Objective and Summary of Qualifications, and appears immediately after your Name and Address. Include three to six points outlining your most relevant strengths for the type of work you are looking for. Describe your competitive advantage, the value you offer. Draw upon your work experience, volunteer and/or extracurricular activities in terms of duration, scope, accomplishments, etc. If you lack relevant experience, emphasize those skills you have developed in terms of interpersonal, organizational, supervisory, etc. Indicate formal or professional training/education. Note if you are bilingual (English/French) or speak other languages. List relevant areas of expertise, e.g., computer proficiency, scientific instrumentation, etc. Draw upon your personal characteristics that are requisites for the position you are seeking, e.g., enthusiastic, flexible, attention to detail.

EDUCATION

Include colleges/universities where you have been awarded a degree (or are where you are working on getting a degree). List the name of your degree (no abbreviations, please) and/or certification that you have obtained, or will obtain, the month and year of your graduation,  and your major and minor(s). If you have received any specific education-related awards, they need to be listed in another section with the exception of Magna Cum Laude or Summa Cum Laude, etc. They can be listed here as it is something that should stand out. List the dates you attended school, too.

If you do not have any college experience, list your high school information. Or, if you just started college and had some related course-work in high school, you can list them here as well.

For students in post secondary education, first year through six months prior to graduation: state Candidate for Degree, Discipline (major/minor), college, and year beginning program: Candidate for Associate Degree of Computer Science. Include GPA if applicable. You may wish to include specialization if applicable. For alumni and students in graduating year: state Degree, Discipline (major/minor), college, and year degree obtained or the month/year degree will be obtained. Add Specialization or Option if you wish: Associate of Arts, History, College, month, and year. Drop reference to the month by the end of the year.

Check the name of the degree you get (Associate of Applied Science in Engineering), and list it preferably unabbreviated. Multiple entries: when referring to additional studies at other schools or to more than one program at Waterloo (Bachelor, Master), arrange entries in reverse chronological order, i.e., most recent first. Co-op students in graduation year may wish to add a statement about co-operative education and alternating work/study periods to explain the jobs in "Work Experience" if you think employers you are applying to are not familiar with co-op education.

RELEVANT COURSES

A sub heading of the Education section. Choose six to ten courses related to your Job Objective where you have not utilized this knowledge yet in a work environment. Do not include course numbers. If the name of the course as listed in the catalog does not adequately convey the information you wish, elaborate to show the relevance. Prioritize the list, or arrange by themes, to avoid a random assortment of names. Place in columns for easy reading.

PROJECT/THESIS

A sub heading of Education. Any relevant project, report, thesis, etc. that you have prepared can be referred to by its title in quotation marks (if the title is sufficiently clear enough to give the reader a feeling for scope), or by using a group of words to show its significance or relevance to the employer.

COMPUTER PROFICIENCY

List both your theoretical and working knowledge. Categorize an extensive background in columns with headings such as Hardware, Operating Systems, Software, and Languages.

WORK EXPERIENCE

The Reverse Chronological style of résumé is the most widely accepted format for outlining work experience. Try this type of format first. If you are not getting your best credentials onto page one, then try the Modified Chronological style. If that still does not help, try the Functional model.

PRESENTING YOUR ACCOMPLISHMENTS

Work Experience

List your job title, the name of the organization you worked for and the dates of your employment. Below this, detail your work-related tasks and accomplishments. Write clearly and use words that command attention, such as: operated, created, ensured, maintained, managed, provided, responded, and so on. List the activities and responsibilities that most closely match the prospective employer's needs first.

Volunteer work should be listed in another section unless it is pertinent to the position you are applying for.

Presenting your accomplishments in the right way may take you from job hunting to job offers. The following are synonyms of "accomplishments".

Achievement

Success	Realization	Goal Fulfillment
Expertise	Attainment	

The easiest definition: when you do something successfully. From an employer's standpoint, <u>it is even better if you can state your achievements in a measurable or quantifiable way</u>. What does that mean? Use numbers whenever you can to state **HOW** you achieved the results you are affirming. For instance, if you increased production of the best selling product at your company, HOW MUCH did you increase it by? Quantify your statements whenever possible.

Your accomplishments distinguish you from your competitors in the job-search process. All things being equal, if a hiring manager were looking at two identical prospective employees who could handle the tasks of the job perfectly well, but one had accomplished more than the other, who do you think is going to get a phone call? State what you can offer in terms that the employer will find exciting.

As mentioned above, use numbers to quantify your success. Also, use words that show action. Some of those words are listed here:

Action Verbs / Keywords

Accelerated	Answered	Automated
Accomplished	Anticipated	Awarded
Achieved	Applied	Balanced
Acquired	Appraised	Began
Acted	Approved	Boosted
Activated	Arbitrated	Briefed
Adapted	Arranged	Budgeted
Addressed	Ascertained	Built
Adjusted	Aspired	Calculated
Administered	Assembled	Captured
Advanced	Assessed	Catalogued
Advertised	Assigned	Centralized
Advised	Assisted	Changed
Advocated	Attained	Chaired
Aided	Audited	Charted
Allocated	Augmented	Checked
Analyzed	Authored	Clarified

Classified	Contracted	Determined
Coached	Contributed	Developed
Collaborated	Controlled	Devised
Collected	Converted	Diagnosed
Combined	Cooperated	Directed
Commanded	Coordinated	Discovered
Communicated	Correlated	Dispatched
Compared	Corresponded	Dispensed
Compiled	Counseled	Displayed
Completed	Created	Dissected
Composed	Critiqued	Distinguished
Computed	Cultivated	Distributed
Conceptualized	Customized	Diversified
Condensed	Cut	Documented
Conducted	Debugged	Doubled
Conferred	Decided	Drafted
Conserved	Decreased	Earned
Consolidated	Delegated	Edited
Constructed	Delivered	Educated
Consulted	Demonstrated	Eliminated
Contacted	Designated	Emphasized
Contained	Designed	Employed
Continued	Detected	Enabled

Enacted	Facilitated	Hired
Encouraged	Familiarized	Honed
Enforced	Fashioned	Hypothesized
Engineered	Finalized	Identified
Enhanced	Fixed	Illustrated
Enlarged	Focused	Imagined
Enlisted	Forecasted	Implemented
Ensured	Formed	Improved
Entertained	Formulated	Improvised
Established	Fostered	Incorporated
Estimated	Found	Increased
Evaluated	Founded	Indexed
Examined	Fulfilled	Indoctrinated
Executed	Furnished	Influenced
Expanded	Gained	Informed
Expedited	Gathered	Initiated
Experimented	Generated	Innovated
Explained	Governed	Inspected
Explored	Guided	Inspired
Expressed	Handled	Installed
Extended	Headed	Instituted
Extracted	Heightened	Instructed
Fabricated	Helped	Insured

Integrated	Marketed	Overcame
Interacted	Maximized	Overhauled
Interpreted	Measured	Oversaw
Interviewed	Mediated	Participated
Introduced	Merged	Performed
Invented	Minimized	Persuaded
Investigated	Mobilized	Photographed
Inventoried	Moderated	Pinpointed
Involved	Modified	Piloted
Issued	Monitored	Pioneered
Joined	Motivated	Placed
Judged	Navigated	Planned
Justified	Negotiated	Predicted
Kept	Netted	Prepared
Launched	Observed	Prescribed
Learned	Obtained	Presented
Lectured	Opened	Presided
Led	Operated	Prevented
Lifted	Ordered	Printed
Located	Orchestrated	Prioritized
Logged	Organized	Processed
Maintained	Originated	Produced
Managed	Outlined	Programmed

Projected	Reduced	Routed
Promoted	Referred	Saved
Proofread	Regulated	Scheduled
Proposed	Rehabilitated	Screened
Protected	Related	Set
Proved	Remodeled	Searched
Provided	Rendered	Secured
Publicized	Reorganized	Selected
Published	Repaired	Separated
Purchased	Replaced	Served
Qualified	Reported	Set up
Questioned	Represented	Shaped
Raised	Researched	Shared
Ran	Reshaped	Simplified
Rated	Resolved	Simulated
Reached	Responded	Sketched
Realized	Restored	Sold
Reasoned	Restructured	Solidified
Received	Retrieved	Solved
Recommended	Reversed	Sorted
Reconciled	Reviewed	Spearheaded
Recorded	Revised	Specialized
Recruited	Revitalized	Specified

Sponsored

Stabilized

Staffed

Standardized

Started

Stimulated

Stored

Streamlined

Strengthened

Structured

Studied

Supervised

Supplied

Supplemented

Supported

Surpassed

Surveyed

Sustained

Synthesized

Systematized

Tabulated

Targeted

Taught

Terminated

Tested

Tightened

Totaled

Tracked

Traded

Trained

Transcribed

Transferred

Transformed

Translated

Transmitted

Traveled

Treated

Trimmed

Tutored

Typed

Uncovered

Undertook

Unified

United

Updated

Upgraded

Used

Utilized

Validated

Verbalized

Verified

Vitalized

Volunteered

Weighed

Widened

Won

Worked

Wrote

Honors/Activities/Achievements/Publications

You may have something that fits into one of the categories listed above or you may not. If you do, identify which word best fits and create that category to match your skills. There are many additional sections you may consider using. One or two should be enough. Just be careful not to use so many that it waters down the focus of the résumé.

There are a lot of activities/achievements that don't fit the bill and are not worth mentioning (for most people).

Awards and Scholarships

State name of award, name of institution award received from, and date. Include important awards from both college and high school in reverse chronological order. Explain the meaning of the recognition if the reader would not understand its significance.

Professional Memberships

List those with some relevance to the jobs to which you are applying.

Publications

List in bibliographic form only those publications that the reader of your résumé would be interested in. Include the work which has been published, has been submitted for publication, and is in progress. Include also the papers you presented as a guest speaker. If your list is lengthy, include only those relevant to your Job Objective by stating the heading as Selected Publications.

Languages: Computer or Foreign

Include those for which you are fluent or have a working knowledge. Indicate if you can speak and/or write the language.

Activities/Volunteer

Volunteer work can be included in different ways, depending on the message you want to give. Include volunteer work in this section if you are demonstrating the breadth of your leisure time activities. If you wish to highlight or emphasize these activities, create a separate heading, e.g., Volunteer  Activities, Volunteer Experience, and Community Service. In this section you can either list the organizations, or you can add to the listing more detail about your contributions, beginning each point with an action verb. You can include your Volunteer Experience before Work Experience in your résumé if it would be to your advantage. If your volunteer activities are as important as your paid work experience, add your information to your Work Experience section, with a volunteer notation, e.g., Assistant to Director (volunteer). In listings for activities, state role (e.g., Member, President), name of organization, dates. Organize in reverse chronological order. State if any positions were elected or appointed. At the bottom of the section include interests such as physical fitness, hobbies, sports or leisure activities. Generally, employers are interested in how you spend your time outside of academics and work, e.g., independent/team activities, as well as your well-roundedness because of the transferability to the work you are applying for. However, when in doubt about including this section, leave it off the résumé.

Don't use them if you don't NEED them. They detract from the true purpose of your résumé if they do not aptly FIT the position you are trying to get.

References and Portfolio

A reference notation such as Professional and Personal References Available upon Request is acceptable. Ask the person you would like to use as a reference for permission to do so, and check out what that individual will say about you if contacted by a prospective employer. Do they see your strengths and weaknesses as you see them? It is important to discuss what that person's response might be to potentially embarrassing questions. A bad reference is a job offer killer! Choose someone who has seen your work in as similar a situation as possible to the job for which you are applying. You do not necessarily need to use your immediate supervisor. Give your references a copy of the relevant résumé(s) for the

type(s) of jobs you are applying to. Type the name, address, telephone number of two or three references on a sheet of paper which you can hand to an employer when asked for reference names. If an employer will require a portfolio, or if you think that one would enhance your application, e.g., graphic design, technical writing, teaching, then add the words, Portfolio Available on Request, to your résumé.

New Focus

If your résumés seem to be taking you down a path similar to your last job(s) and you want to change direction, you need to interpret or reformat your past jobs in terms of the duties and

Make Your Résumé Great: A Passion Driven Job Search

responsibilities that characterize the new work you would like to have.

Résumé Building Experience

One of the best ways to find out if a particular type of work is suited to you is to do it. There are several ways: part-time or full-time paid work, short-term or long-term volunteer work. The auspices can be through co-operative education, casual, summer, contract, on-going (permanent), work study, internship, or volunteer positions. In addition to the job content knowledge you gain, there are extra benefits:

- referrals for future jobs through a network that you build
- knowledge of the strengths and weaknesses of your work related skills
- development of communication, leadership, analytical, organizational, problem solving and creative skills
- demonstration of your initiative, and establishment of a track record, for potential employers.

Whatever your job is, take time to reflect on your experiences. Write your thoughts in a journal to keep a permanent record. What is the work being done, how is the work being done, when, how quickly, by whom, using what technology tools. What interpersonal relationships are there that help or impede progress, what are you having fun doing, what do you find boring. Are your surroundings and interactions typical of the workplace you want for your career related job or has this work experience raised a question about your program of academic studies. When it comes time to choose your next series of courses, broaden your investigation into what's available. Is there something even more suited to your present needs and the direction you are choosing to go? With a complete analysis of your experiential learning, you will have data and examples for your next résumé, portfolio, and job interview.

Community Service

Civic and social organizations, whether local, national or international in scope, provide opportunities for individuals to give back something to society. You are able to support a community service compatible with your beliefs and geared toward your leisure needs. It is important that you make the same  type of commitment to the organization as you would to your employer. The organization will be counting on you to do the job as

Make Your Résumé Great: A Passion Driven Job Search

conscientiously as a paid employee. Determine what you would like to contribute to the organization and what knowledge and skills you want to gain.

List 3-5 organizations or community needs that you are interested in helping. Interview the person in charge to determine if your goals and theirs are compatible, and if working together will meet both your needs. When you have made a decision on where you would like to volunteer, agree upon the number of hours, the times you will be available, your specific duties and responsibilities, any training you require, and your out-of-pocket expenses. Having a written, signed contract will alleviate any misunderstandings which might jeopardize your reputation in the future and impact being able to earn good references.

Co-operative Education

Co-operative education provides you with the opportunity to have paid employment in positions that complement your academic program. Alternating work and study terms takes somewhat longer than the traditional method of study with a summer break. Co-op positions are full-time, usually for 4-8 months, or 1 year. The advantage for you is in having a formal structure through which you can try out different jobs to see what you like and are good at. With regular performance evaluations by your supervisors, you can acquire

Make Your Résumé Great: A Passion Driven Job Search

an employer's perspective on how well you measure up to the quality of other people working in that position. You can begin to see your competitive advantage. By taking positions with increasing levels of responsibility, you will have a solid résumé with which to approach the job market for a full-time position.

Summer, Contract, On-going (Permanent)

Jobs in these categories usually are offered on a full-time basis, ranging from 25-30 hours or more a week. Seen as building blocks to lay the foundation for your career, working in a diversity of settings will enable you to experience personally, as well as observe, aspects of employment. By testing, you will come to know what you like and don't like, what you're good at and what areas you need to develop expertise. For those of you in an academic program that is not specifically preparing you for employment as does mechanical engineering, health promotion, or accounting, you are receiving the added benefits of gaining work related skills that employers are seeking.

Work Study

Within an academic environment, there may be positions funded by governments, for up to 10 hours a week over the term, to help students finance their education. Carefully read the job notices. If the information is vague, phone the person who would be hiring for the position for more details. Work study can be a good way to apply your knowledge in different settings. In addition to helping you clarify your career goals and secure references, you can end up with excellent transferable skills.

Internship

An internship gives you an opportunity to have a structured experience combining work and learning in a field you are considering for your career. The work is usually unpaid, although you may find some positions with a stipend or an hourly rate typical for that kind of job. The work can be part-time during an academic term, a full-time block during the weeks between terms, full-time for an academic term or longer. A professor from your faculty may oversee the work in conjunction with your employer so that appropriate academic credit can be given. Even if you succeed in obtaining an internship that will not result in academic credit, the experience is invaluable in exploring career possibilities, gaining work skills valued in the marketplace, and obtaining references.

Volunteer

Volunteering allows you to check out many types of work. Some examples are: animal care, environmental preservation, health education, marketing, computer programming. You may want to undertake a special project as a class assignment in a course. Rather than proceeding only through the theoretical perspective to obtain your academic grade, perhaps you could locate a group who could benefit from your work.

Anyone can volunteer in practically any organization. Look through the files and directories in the Career Center. The two questions you need to answer for yourself are: what would you like to give to the community and what would you like to get back in return. For anyone not able to obtain paid employment to learn about the work world and expand employable skills, volunteering is beneficial.

REFLECTION NOTES

Make Your Résumé Great: A Passion Driven Job Search

REFLECTION NOTES

Make Your Résumé Great: A Passion Driven Job Search

REFLECTION NOTES

Make Your Résumé Great: A Passion Driven Job Search

REFLECTION NOTES

Chapter 5

MAKE YOUR
RÉSUMÉ GREAT

Make Your Résumé Great: A Passion Driven Job Search

Chapter 5

MAKING A RÉSUMÉ GREAT

THINGS TO REMEMBER ABOUT THE RÉSUMÉ

- It is not a type of document that you can make once and forget about. You will update it from time to time as needed.
- There is a directly proportional relationship between how it looks and how much time you have spent working on it.

- It is a marketing tool. It tells others about you and attempts to "sell" the employer on the idea that YOU are the best person for the position.
- It is your best bet for getting hired – no matter what your field is.
- If you don't spend your time NOW making yours the best it can be, you will either spend the time LATER working on it, or you will pay someone else (who doesn't know you) to write it for you.

When you *write your own résumé*, not only are you able to make the important decisions about what gets included and what does not, but there is a HUGE payoff when it comes time to interview.

Make Your Résumé Great: A Passion Driven Job Search

During the course of an interview, you will be asked a number of questions about your background. By taking the time to review your qualifications, you will be much better prepared for the interview. You will have the confidence that comes from being certain of your skills and abilities. This may be one of the best résumé tips you ever read.

Additional résumé tips to consider when writing your résumé:

1. Keep your statements to one or two sentences. Anything longer than that and the person reading your résumé may lose interest.

2. Effectively use the "white space" on your page. Guide the reader down the page, providing an occasional break for the eyes.

3. Collect the information you need before actually writing the document itself. Do not "wing it". Prepare, plan, <u>then place</u> your accomplishments and such on paper.

4. Your entire employment history does not need to be listed. Only note the most current positions you have held. Depending upon how much you have moved from job to job, that could be two employers or it

could be five. Do not feel the need to re-create the last thirteen years on paper, though.

5. Write professionally, avoiding jargon or slang.

6. Revise, revise, and revise. Make this piece of paper work for YOU.

7. Using graphics can add that extra touch to get your résumé noticed. Especially when applying for a position in a creative field, graphics can set you above the rest. Fashion designers, graphic designers, animators, and artists usually do not follow the black and white résumé trend. When applying for these creative jobs, consider a number of ways to make your résumé special. Use decorative or colored paper, but make sure that your text is still clear to read over the background. You can use images on your résumé to highlight your accomplishments as a photographer, animator, or the like.

For more traditional, formal résumés, logos and decoration should be subtler. The header can include a dash of color or a different font. Bullets don't need to be the typical solid dot. Instead, use a pencil icon if you are applying for a teaching job or a computer mouse if you want to work in IT. Some professional certification boards allow for their logos to be used on résumés, so this could highlight your skills. Charts as well could organize your résumé in a creative and unusual way. Graphics are less acceptable in formal résumés than in creative résumés, so choose wisely. A small touch of

133

creativity can be beneficial, but too much will make your résumé unreadable.

This list is to help ensure that you are presenting yourself in the best possible light. If your résumé is not doing these five things, it might need some extra attention. Making a résumé great is vital if you are to beat out your competition.

1. Your résumé should show the prospective employer that you know how to spell and use appropriate grammar. Check for typos, spelling errors and tense consistency. (Don't switch from past to present tense.) When your résumé looks professional, the employer makes an assumption that you are a professional, too.

2. Show your enthusiasm! You want the employer to sit up and take notice. Energy and excitement are contagious. When the employer reads your résumé, he/she should feel as though you will start the job on day 1 with an attitude of "Let's get to work now!"

3. Give the employer the information necessary to provide an excellent picture of what you have done in the past, but don't add so many details that the résumé gets bogged down. Employers want relevant information, but they do not want to be inundated with every aspect of every position you held. They are not especially concerned if you opened the mail or filed personnel records.

Make Your Résumé Great: A Passion Driven Job Search

Along with this is the use of "white space". Reading résumés can be tedious, especially when they are so full of words that there is no break - or "white space" - for the eyes to rest. Carefully choose the qualifications listed on your résumé so that your résumé won't be so full of information that there is no space for the reader's eyes to take a break.

4. Exclude all personal information, such as weight, height, age, etc... It probably will not help your chances at all. If anything, it has the potential to eliminate you from some organizations, some jobs or perhaps in the minds of some people. For example, say you include information about your political preferences. If you happen to send your résumé to a hiring manager who believes completely the opposite of you, it's very possible that your résumé will not get the attention it deserves. Is that fair? No. Does it happen? Yes.

5. Of all the things to proofread again, look at your contact information. Make sure your phone number(s) and email addresses are accurate. One wrong number or letter and you might never know what you missed. Read: If the employer cannot contact you, you will not get interviewed.

VITAL RÉSUMÉ DO'S AND DON'TS

Your résumé may be about you, but the employer thinks it's about them...the company. They look at your qualifications and ponder just what you have that they might need. Will you fit in with their corporate climate? How long will it take you to contribute to the bottom line?

If you follow the Résumé Do's and Don'ts lists below, you will have a much better chance of writing a résumé to which employers immediately relate.

The Do List

1. Focus on the employer's needs, not on your own. You have to clearly address your accomplishments and skills in a way that an employer will want to find out more about you. (Read: Call you for an interview)

2. Keep your résumé as short and sweet as possible. Remember that an employer is only likely to scan it for a few short seconds. It has to pack a punch right away. Use Action Keywords to bring your résumé to life.

3. Proofread what you have typed. Proofread it again. Have your best friend look it over, and then have your parents take a look at it. The more people who proofread it, the more likely you are to ensure it's free of typos and grammar errors.

4. *You can't proofread too much!*

5. Use <u>quantifiable</u> accomplishments wherever possible. If you increased revenues at the Super 24 Movie Complex, determine the extent to which you contributed to the monthly increase and use that number in your résumé. People like numbers. If you saved the Mr. Friendly Syrup Company money by finding a better way to package their syrup, then find out how much was saved and state that.

6. Use good quality paper. Keep the color neutral, such as white or ivory. Linen paper, paper with watermarks and those with heavier weight (at least 24lb or higher) are great choices.

THE RÉSUMÉ CHECKLIST

As you revise your résumé, review this checklist and ensure you are presenting yourself in the best possible light and help you eliminate errors. This is not an exhaustive list, but it does offer some beneficial points ideas you might not have considered.

1. Proofread again and again. Check for grammar, spelling errors and consistency. Be especially consistent in typing every accomplishment

Make Your Résumé Great: A Passion Driven Job Search

and every activity in the past tense. Do not switch from past to present tense.

2. Do not use the pronoun "I". Just don't.

3. Show your enthusiasm! You want the employer to sit up and take notice. Energy and excitement are contagious.

4. If you go into too much detail about your work experience, you will bore the reader to death. Employers want relevant information, but they don't want to be inundated with every aspect of the position you held. They are not especially concerned if you opened the mail or filed personnel records.

5. Are you using good quality paper? White, off white, off white…you get the idea. Make sure it is at least 24 lb paper.

6. Exclude all personal information, such as weight, height, age, etc.. It probably will not help your chances at all. If anything, it has the potential to be a sticking point with someone for some reason. No, it shouldn't. No, it's not fair. It is, however, the real world and it does happen.

7. Does your résumé have a clear and concise Objective Statement? If it doesn't, you probably ought to consider it, unless you have a good reason not to. A good reason might be that you are working with a headhunter who happens to loathe Objective Statements. Ok. If you need to know more about the Job Objective, click on the link to take you to that area of the site.

8. Have you told the truth? Presenting your accomplishments and skills in the best possible light is highly recommended. If you start leaning toward stretching the truth, then you might be crossing a very important line. What line? Oh, the line that determines whether you might get fired or not.

9. Does the overall layout of your résumé look pleasing to the eye? That is a hard thing to qualify, yes. Having someone else give you their opinion might be the best approach here. After all, you have looked at this piece of paper for days or weeks by now, right?

10. Of all the things to proofread again, look at your contact information. Make sure your phone number(s) and email addresses are accurate. One wrong number or letter and you might never know what you missed. That sounds strange, but you get the idea, I hope.

THE RÉSUMÉ QUIZ

Take this Résumé Quiz to see what you have learned so far.

The Quiz

1. What is a résumé?

a. love story

b. a job application

c. a marketing tool

2. What is more important in a résumé?

a. your list of references

b. where you live

c. your skill set

3. How long does an employer scan a résumé?

a. 5 minutes

b. 2 minutes

c. less than 1 minute

4. What is the résumé objective statement?

a. job salary

b. job offer

c. job target

5. Who is the best person to write your résumé?

a. a commercial résumé service

b. your mom

c. You

6. How many revisions does a great résumé go through?

a. 25

b. 1

c. somewhere in between

7. Which of the three items below should NOT be on the résumé?

Make Your Résumé Great: A Passion Driven Job Search

a. your skills and
accomplishments

b. your address

c. your hair color

8. Why is writing your own
résumé important?

a. you need to practice your
typing skills

b. writing someone else's would
be difficult

c. you will do much better when
interviewing

9. A résumé should focus on
the needs of…

a. your younger sibling

b. anyone but you

c. the employer

10. Which one of the
following words is NOT an
action word?

a. managed

b. negotiated

c. chicken

Résumé Quiz Answer Key:

If you answered anything other than "c" for any of the above questions, you either have a great sense of humor or don't "get it".

In all sincerity, while this was a fun little résumé quiz, it is meant to convey some of the realities of the résumé-writing process.

First, understand the big picture. You want to find a career that will be satisfying to you and will provide you with the opportunities you seek. Set some goals that will help you achieve success in the job-search process as well as direct your steps as you head into the future. Don't just focus on the short-term goal of finding a job. Find the RIGHT job.

Second, while this whole process is somewhat serious in nature, keep a smile on your face and find humor wherever you can. It is easy to get so wrapped up in revising your résumé for the 5th time that you get somewhat surly, but back away when you can and have some fun with it, too.

Smarter Résumés: A Passion Driven Job Search

REFLECTION NOTES

Smarter Résumés: A Passion Driven Job Search

REFLECTION NOTES

Smarter Résumés: A Passion Driven Job Search

REFLECTION NOTES

Smarter Résumés: A Passion Driven Job Search

REFLECTION NOTES

Chapter 6

THE JOB

APPLICATION PROCESS

Smarter Résumés: A Passion Driven Job Search

Smarter Résumés: A Passion Driven Job Search

Chapter 6

The Job Application Process

A completed job application provides an employer with information about your educational preparation, work experience, and personal characteristics. A job application form is designed to provide information about you as a prospective employee. It is important that the application form is completed neatly and completely. The application should offer the employer a positive statement about you as a person and communicate your value as an employee.

The application tells the employer more than just information about your education, work experience, and skills you bring to the job. An employer will also get an understanding of your ability to follow directions, work neatly, spell correctly, and provide accurate and complete data.

The application is a legal document and you can be fired for not completing it honestly. However, it is important to focus on your strengths and present all information in the most positive way possible.

More Helpful Information

Job Application. Try this exercise to refresh your memory regarding the function of a job application.

http://www.aitech.ac.jp/~iteslj/quizzes/employ/applic.htm

Online Job Fairs

Best Jobs U.S.A.

http://www.bestjobsusa.com/sections/CAN-careerfairs/index.asp

Recourse Communications, Inc. (specializing in human resources and recruiting over 27 years) launched this site offering access to their database of thousands of jobs from a wide range of industries, which have included corporate profiles, post your résumé, and find info on career fairs and employment events nationwide. Career Guide is great resource for links to other employment web sites.

CareerMart

http://www.careermart.com/

This allows you to satisfy your entire job hunting needs in one place. Learn job listings, about employers, home pages of leading companies or conduct a job search. Post your résumé where employers meet daily to find qualified applicants. College Info Center includes info about campus interviews, job fairs and college events.

Career Fair Online

http://résumégenie.com/careers.asp?hl=Career%20Fair%20Online

Find job listings.

JobBankUSA.com!

http://www.jobbankusa.com/

Everything you need to find, start and

grow into your next job. JobBank USA Specializes in providing

employment and résumé information services to job candidates,

employers and recruitment firms.

Jobs.Com

http://www.jobs.com

Provides information on job listings, company profiles, and hosts

virtual job fairs.

Job Web Catapult

http://www.jobweb.org/catapult/catapult.htm

This site provides job related information and hosts a job fair.

IT IS THE REAL YOU.

So enjoy who you are and relate it in the best possible way to

employers. All that you have attained in times past will propel you

into the future with an assurance of continued success.

The Don't List

1. Lie. Just tell the truth. By all means, present your achievements in the best possible light, but be careful about stretching the truth. If you don't tell the truth, it will likely come back to haunt you. You may not be able to perform the functions of the job very well and get yourself fired. The truth may come out at some point and according to company regulations, you guessed it, you get yourself fired. It's not worth it.

2. Be repetitious. If you performed a specific task at more than one job, list it in one place only. The employer only needs to know that you are capable of handling something, not that you have done it more than once. Find something else that the employer can benefit from knowing about you and include that instead.

3. Rule out volunteer work. Consider non-paid positions where you made a contribution. You probably learned a lot from volunteering at a local charity or from the office you held in the district PTA. Those are valuable insights into your character and the employer will be glad to read about them in your résumé.

4. Create your own résumé format. The formats that are in use exist for a reason...they work. If you are considering starting your own résumé trend, let's just pause a moment and reflect on why that is such a bad idea. Ok, the moment is over. Use the prescribed formats and save yourself some time and hassle.

5. Rush through this whole process. You will have a much more effective résumé if you take the time to do it right. How does that phrase go? If you don't have the time to do something right, you probably don't have the time to do it over. You can do this! You know you better than anyone else – and that's all you need to get this task completed!

Here are four tips to help you make your résumé stand out:

First, use keywords into your résumé to embolden it. Use words that show action as well as words which are common to your particular field. Many companies use software to  review résumés and search for keywords. If your résumé doesn't have the right ones or have them in the right amounts, you won't get selected for an interview.

Smarter Résumés: A Passion Driven Job Search

Second, make sure you use a job objective to clarify exactly what it is you are looking for and how you will be an asset to the organization. Don't assume it will be clear to someone who reads your résumé. Be clear and be concise. A job objective will rarely ever work against you, but if you don't have one and the employer can't figure out exactly what it is you're looking for, you're dead in the water.

Third, use white space to your advantage. Don't make your résumé so busy that it wearies the eyes of the reader. Allow for breaks between paragraphs and sections.

Fourth and last, use the best quality paper that you can afford. Actually, if you can't afford outstanding paper, find someone from whom you can borrow money and buy the best paper you can find. It will be worth it. Make it look good - and that means white, opaque, linen paper.

So, now you have a pretty good idea of what you need to do to make sure your résumé looks as good as possible. Use this information (and the rest of the information on this web site) to your advantage. If you are going to write a résumé, you might as well write an excellent one. Make your résumé stand out – write it right!

Smarter Résumés: A Passion Driven Job Search

REFLECTION NOTES

REFLECTION NOTES

REFLECTION NOTES

Smarter Résumés: A Passion Driven Job Search

REFLECTION NOTES

Smarter Résumés: A Passion Driven Job Search

Chapter 7

COVER LETTERS, TYPES, AND EXAMPLES

Smarter Résumés: A Passion Driven Job Search

Smarter Résumés: A Passion Driven Job Search

Chapter 7

COVER LETTERS: TYPES AND EXAMPLES

When you write your résumé and cover letter – and even in an interview – expressing your achievements is extremely important. The employer needs to know that you did more than simply complete a variety of tasks. Don't be shy here. Be bold (not arrogant) in asserting your ability to realize goals, gain expertise in certain areas and succeed at what you do.

Why do employers place such an emphasis on accomplishments?

Think of it this way: Many people can perform tasks. How many of them look for improve their own work environment? How many attempt to help their boss succeed? **The person who goes above and beyond** the "call of duty" is the one that employers are especially looking for.

Communicating your accomplishments to an employer goes beyond simply stating the skills you have. It describes <u>HOW WELL</u> you utilize the skills and abilities you have. For instance, let's say you are an automotive mechanic. You diagnose and repair engines using computer diagnostics. But let's say you also focus extra time and energy on mastering the ability to repair ignition problems. You may have even won an award at your last job for doing just that. The employer wants to know what you have done that goes above and beyond what is normally expected of you. **Blow your own horn!** (Please forgive the pun.)

Think about everything you accomplish each day at your job and how you demonstrate your proficiency at various tasks. What makes you so good at what you do? How are you able to exhibit your determination to succeed? Dig a bit into the whys and hows of your job and how you do so well and you will start to understand the essence of true achievement.

As you create a list of your accomplishments, you will get an extra benefit from going through this process.

You will feel more confident about yourself.

Keep all of these good vibes with you while you are writing your résumé, your cover letter AND as you interview. The positive flow of energy that will emanate from you will be so contagious that the hiring manager will take notice of you immediately. Everyone likes to be around someone who is self-assured and energetic. What is the best part of all of this? No blue smoke and mirrors were needed to create this scene. It's all you.

The guidelines here apply to both hard copy correspondence and e-mail.

Main **differences** between e-mail and hard copy correspondence:

Format: your **signature block** (address, etc.) goes below your name in e-mail, while it goes at the top of the page on hard copy.

E-mail requires a **subject line** logical to the recipient. E-mail subject lines can make or break whether your e-mail is opened and read. Hard copy can have a subject line too, but it's on the letter (after recipient's address block and before "Dear...," and it's seen after the letter is opened.

Signature: Of course you won't have a handwritten signature on e-mail, but don't forget this on hard copy.

ALL COVER LETTERS SHOULD:

Explain why you are sending a résumé.

- Don't send a résumé without a cover letter.

Don't make the reader guess what you are asking for; be specific: Do you want a summer internship opportunity, or a permanent position at graduation; are you inquiring about future employment possibilities?

Tell specifically how you learned about the position or the organization

- a flyer posted in your department, a web site, a family friend who works at the organization. It is appropriate to mention the name of someone who suggested that you write.

Convince the reader to look at your résumé.

- The cover letter will be seen first.
Therefore, it must be very well written and targeted to that employer.

Call **attention to elements of your background**

- education, leadership, experience — that are relevant to a position you are seeking. Be as specific as possible, using examples.

Reflect your attitude, personality, enthusiasm, and communication skills.

Provide or refer to any information specifically requested in a job advertisement that might not be covered in your résumé, such as availability date, or reference to an attached writing sample.

Indicate what you will do to follow-up.
In a letter of application\

- applying for an advertised opening — applicants often say something like "I look forward to hearing from you." However, if you have

Smarter Résumés: A Passion Driven Job Search

further contact info (e.g. phone number) and if the employer hasn't said "no phone calls," it's better to take the initiative to follow-up, saying something like, "I will contact you in the next two weeks to see if you require any additional information regarding my qualifications."

In a letter of inquiry

- asking about the possibility of an opening — don't assume the employer will contact you. You should say something like, "I will contact you in two weeks to learn more about upcoming employment opportunities with (name of organization)." Then mark your calendar to make the call.

PAGE MARGINS, FONT STYLE AND SIZE

For hard copy, left and right page margins of one to 1.5 inches generally look good. You can adjust your margins to balance how your document looks on the page.

Use a font style that is simple, clear and commonplace, such as Times New Roman, Arial or Calibri. Font SIZES from 10-12 points are generally in the ballpark of looking appropriate. Keep in mind that **different font styles in the same point size are not the same size**. A 12-point Arial is larger than a 12-point Times New Roman.

If you are having trouble fitting a document on one page, sometimes a slight margin and/or font adjustment can be the solution.

Serif or sans serif? Sans (without) serif fonts are those like Arial and Calibri that don't have the small finishing strokes on the ends of each letter. There is a great deal of research and debate on the pros and cons of each. Short story: use what you like, within reason; note what employers use; generally sans serif fonts are used for on-monitor reading and serif fonts are used for lengthly print items (like books); serif fonts may be considered more formal. Test: ask someone to look at a document for five seconds; take away the document; ask the person what font was on the document; see if s/he even noticed the style. A too-small or too-large font gets noticed, as does a weird style.

Should your résumé and cover letter font style and size match? It can be a nice touch to look polished. But it's also possible to have polished documents that are not in matching fonts. A significant difference in style and size might be noticed. Remember that you can have your documents reviewed through advising, and that might be a fine-tuning question you ask.

SAMPLE COVER LETTER FORMAT GUIDELINES:

*(Hard copy: sender address and contact info at top. **Your address and the date can be left-justified, or centered**.)*

Your Street Address
City, State Zip Code
Telephone Number
E-mail Address

Month, Day, Year

Mr./Ms./Dr. First Name Last Name
Title
Name of Organization
Street or P. O. Box Address
City, State Zip Code

Dear Mr./Ms./Dr. Last Name:

Opening paragraph: State why you are writing; how you learned of the organization or position, and basic information about yourself.

2nd paragraph: Tell why you are interested in the employer or type of work the employer does (Simply stating that you are interested does not tell why, and can sound like a form letter). Demonstrate that you know enough about the employer or position to relate your background to the employer or position. Mention specific qualifications which make you a good fit for the employer's needs. (Focus on what you can do for the employer, not what the employer can do for you.) This is an opportunity to explain in more detail relevant items in your résumé. Refer to the fact that your résumé is enclosed. Mention other enclosures if such are required to apply for a position.

3rd paragraph: Indicate that you would like the opportunity to interview for a position or to talk with the employer to learn more about their opportunities or hiring plans. State what you will do to follow up, such as telephone the employer within two weeks. If you will be in the employer's location and could offer to schedule a visit, indicate when. State that you would be glad to provide the employer with any additional information needed. Thank the employer for her/his consideration.

Sincerely,

(Your handwritten signature [on hard copy])

Your name typed
(In case of e-mail, your full contact info appears below your printed name [instead of at the top, as for hard copy], and of course there is no handwritten signature)

Enclosure(s) (refers to résumé, etc.)

***(Note: the contents of your letter might best be arranged into four paragraphs. Consider what you need to say and use good writing style.** See the following examples for Creations in organization and layout.)*

INFORMATION-SEEKING LETTERS AND FOLLOW-UP

To draft an effective cover letter, you need to indicate that you know something about the employing organization. Sometimes, even with research efforts, you don't have enough information to do this. In such a case it is appropriate to write requesting information.

After you receive the desired information you can then draft a follow-up letter that:

Thanks the sender for the information;

Markets why you would be a good job candidate for that organization based on the information; and

Explains why you are sending your résumé.

....which means it does what all cover letters should do, as explained at the start above.

Letter of application, hard copy version

E-2 Apartment Heights Dr.
Charleston, SC 29401
(843) 555-0101
abcd@yahoo.com

February 22, 2011

Dr. Michelle Rhodes
Principal, Wolftrap Elementary School
1205 Beulah Road
Vienna, SC 22182

Dear Dr. Baylor:

I enjoyed our conversation on February 18th at the Family and Child

Development seminar on teaching elementary children and appreciated your personal input about balancing the needs of children and the community during difficult economic times. This letter is to follow-up about the Fourth Grade Teacher position as discussed at the seminar. I will complete my M.Ed. in Curriculum and Instruction at Virginia Tech in May 2011, and will be available for employment as soon as needed for the 2011-12 school year.

My teacher preparation program at Virginia Tech has included a full academic year of student teaching. Last semester I taught second grade and this semester am teaching fourth grade. These Available experiences have afforded me the opportunity to:

- Develop lesson plans on a wide range of topics and class levels of academic ability,
- Work with emotionally and physically challenged students in a total inclusion program,
- Observe and participate in effective classroom management approaches,
- Assist with parent-teacher conferences, and
- Complete in-service sessions on diversity, math and reading skills, and community relations.

My experience includes work in a prison day care facility, Rainbow Riders Childcare Center, and in Virginia Tech's Child Development Laboratory. Both these facilities are NAEYC-accredited and adhere to the highest standards. At both locations, I led small and large group activities, helped with lunches and snacks, and implemented appropriate activities. Both experiences also provided me with extensive exposure to the implementation of developmentally appropriate activities and materials.

I enthusiastically look forward to putting my knowledge and experience into practice in the public school system. Next week I will be in Vienna, and I plan to call you then to answer any questions that you may have. I can be reached before then at (843) 555-7670. Thank you very much for your consideration.

Sincerely,
(handwritten signature)
Betty Wilkins

Enclosure

Letter of application, e-mail version

Subject line: *(logical to recipient!)* Application for sales representative for mid-Atlantic area

April 14, 2012

Mr. William Miller
Employment Manager
ABC Pharmaceutical Corporation
13764 Jefferson Parkway
Columbia, SC 28901
jackson@ABCpharmaceutical.com

Dear Mr. Miller:

From the ABC web site I learned about your need for a sales representative for the Virginia, Maryland, and North Carolina areas. I am very interested in this position with ABC Pharmaceuticals, and believe that my education and employment background are appropriate for the position.

You indicate that a requirement for the position is a track record of success in meeting sales goals. I have done this. After completion of my B.S. in biology, and prior to beginning my master's degree in marketing, I worked for two years as a sales representative with a regional whole foods company. My efforts yielded success in new business development, and my sales volume consistently met or exceeded company goals. I would like to repeat that success in the pharmaceutical industry, using my academic background in science and business. I will complete my M.S. in marketing in mid-May and will be available to begin employment in early June.

Attached is a copy of my résumé, which more fully details my qualifications for the position.

I look forward to talking with you regarding sales opportunities with ABC Pharmaceuticals. Within the next week I will contact you to confirm that you received my e-mail and résumé and to answer any questions you may have.

Thank you very kindly for your consideration.

Sincerely,
Taylor L. Davis
5542 Hunt Club Lane, #1
Charleston, SC 29401
(843) 555-8082
lajohnson@yahoo.com

Résumé attached as MS Word document *(assuming company web site instructed applicants to do this)*

Letter of application, e-mail version

Subject line: *(logical to recipient!)* Application for marketing research position #031210-528

March 14, 2012

Ms. Charlene Prince
Director of Personnel
Large National Bank Corporation
Roanoke, SC 24040
cprince@largebank.com

Dear Ms. Taylor:

As I indicated in our telephone conversation yesterday, I would like to apply for the marketing research position (#031210-528) advertised in the March 12th *Roanoke Times and World News*. With my undergraduate research background, my training in psychology and sociology, and my work experience, I believe I could make an Available contribution to Large National Bank Corporation in this position.

In May I will complete my B.S. in Psychology with a minor in Sociology at Virginia Tech. As part of the requirements for this degree, I am involved in a senior marketing research project that has given me experience interviewing and surveying research subjects and assisting with the analysis of the data collected. I also have completed a course in statistics and research methods.

My experience also includes working part-time as a bookkeeper in a small independent bookstore with an annual budget of approximately $150,000. Because of the small size of this business, I have been exposed to and participated in most aspects of managing a business, including advertising and marketing. As the bookkeeper, I produced monthly sales reports that allow the owner/buyer to project seasonal inventory needs. I also assisted with the development of ideas for special promotional events and calculated book sales proceeds after each event in order to escalate its success.

I believe my combination of business experience and social science research training is an excellent match for the marketing research position you described. Enclosed is a copy of my résumé with additional information about my qualifications. Thank you very much for your consideration. I look forward to receiving your reply.

Sincerely,
Perry Alexander
250 Prices Fork Road
Charleston, SC 29401
(843) 555-1234
alex.lawrence@yahoo.com

Résumé attached as MS Word document

Letter of application, hard copy version

1000 Terrace View Apts.
Charleston, SC 29401
(843) 555-4523
stevemason@gmail.com

March 25, 2012

Janice Wilson
Personnel Director
Anderson Construction Company

3507 Rockville Pike
Rockville, MD 20895

Dear Ms. Wilson:

I read in the March 24th *Washington Post* classified section of your need for a Civil Engineer or Building Construction graduate for one of your Washington, DC, area sites. I will be returning to the Washington area after graduation in May and believe that I have the necessary credentials for the project.

Every summer for the last five years I have worked at several levels in the construction industry. As indicated on my enclosed résumé, I have worked as a general laborer, and moved up to skilled carpentry work, and last summer served as assistant construction manager on a two million dollar residential construction project.

In addition to this practical experience, I will complete requirements for my B.S. in Building Construction in May. As you may know, Virginia Tech is one of the few universities in the country that offers such a specialized degree for the construction industry. I am confident that my degree, along with my years of construction industry experience, makes me an excellent candidate for your job.

The Anderson Construction Company projects are familiar to me, and my aspiration is to work for a company that has your excellent reputation. I would welcome the opportunity to interview with you. I will be in the Washington area during the week of April 12th and would be available to speak with you at that time. In the next week to ten days I will contact you to answer any questions you may have.

Thank you for your consideration.

Sincerely,
(handwritten signature)

Smarter Résumés: A Passion Driven Job Search

Jesse Mason

Enclosure

Letter of inquiry about employment possibilities, e-mail version

Subject: *(logical to recipient!)* Inquiry about software engineering position after completion of M.S. in computer engineering

December 12, 2009

Mr. Robert Burns
President, Template Division
MEGATEK Corporation
9845 Technical Way
Arlington, SC 22207
burns@megatek.com

Dear Mr. Burns:

Via online research in Hokies4Hire through Career Services at Virginia Tech, I learned of MEGATEK. Next May I will complete my master of science in computer engineering. From my research on your web site, I believe there would be a good fit between my skills and interests and your needs. I am interested in a software engineering position upon completion of my degree.

As a graduate student, I am one of six members on a software development team in which we are writing a computer-aided aircraft design program for NASA. My responsibilities include designing, coding, and testing of a graphical portion of the program which requires the use of ZX-WWG for graphics input and output. I have a strong background in CAD, software development, and engineering, and believe that these skills would benefit the designing and manufacturing aspects of template software. Enclosed is my résumé with further background information.

My qualifications equip me to make a contribution to the project areas in which your division of MEGATEK is expanding efforts. I would appreciate the opportunity to discuss a position with you, and will contact you in a week or ten days to answer any questions you may have and to see if you need any other information from me. Thank you for your consideration.

Sincerely,
Stevens McIntire
123 Ascot Lane
Charleston, SC 29401
(843) 555-2556
mcintires@yahoo.com

Résumé attached as MS Word document

Letter of inquiry about internship opportunities, hard copy version

2343 Blankinship Road
Charleston, SC 29401
(843) 555-2233
LeeGamble@yahoo.com

January 12, 2012

Ms. Sylvia Range

Special Programs Assistant
Marion County Family Court Wilderness Challenge
303 Center Street
Marion, SC 24560

Subject: Wilderness Challenge internship position

Dear Ms. Range:

This semester I am a junior at Virginia Tech, working toward my bachelor's degree in family and child development. I am seeking an internship for this summer 2012, and while researching opportunities in the field of criminal justice and law, I found that your program works with juvenile delinquents. I am writing to inquire about possible internship opportunities with the Marion County Family Court Wilderness Challenge.

My work background and coursework have supplied me with many skills and an understanding of dealing with the adolescent community; for example:

- 10 hours per week as a volunteer hotline assistant for a local intervention center. After a 50-hour training program, I counseled teenagers about personal concerns and referred them, when necessary, to appropriate professional services for additional help.

- Residence hall assistant in my residence hall, which requires me to establish rapport with fifty residents and advise them on personal matters, as well as university policies. In addition, I develop social and educational programs and activities each semester for up to 200 participants.

My enclosed résumé provides additional details about my background.

Smarter Résumés: A Passion Driven Job Search

I will be in the Marion area during my spring break, March 6-10. I will call you next week to see if it would be possible to meet with you in early March to discuss your program.

Thank you for your consideration.

Sincerely,
(handwritten signature)
Lee Gamble

Enclosure

Information seeking letter, hard copy version

23 Roanoke Street
Charleston, SC 29401
(843) 555-1123
SamanthaWatts@yahoo.com

October 23, 2012

Mr. James G. Webb
Delon Hampton & Associates
800 K Street, N.W., Suite 720
Washington, DC 20001-8000

Dear Mr. Webb:

Next May I will complete my bachelor's degree in Architecture at Virginia Tech, and am researching employment opportunities in the Washington area. I obtained your name from Professor (Last Name) who teaches my professional seminar class this semester. S/he indicated that you had volunteered to provide highly motivated graduating students with career advice, and I hope that your schedule will permit you to allow me to ask for some of your time and advice. I am particularly interested in historic preservation and have done research on the DHA website to learn that your firm does work in this area. I am also interested in learning how the architects in your firm began their careers. My résumé is enclosed simply to give you some information about my background and project work.

Within two weeks I will call you to arrange a time to speak to you by telephone or perhaps visit your office if that would be convenient. I will be in the Washington area during the week of November 22. I very much appreciate your time and consideration of my request, and I look forward to talking with you.

Sincerely,
(handwritten signature)
Samantha Watts

Follow-up letter to information seeking meeting, e-mail version

Subject: *(logical to recipient!)* Thank you for meeting Tuesday, Nov. 23

November 26, 2012

Mr. James G. Webb
Delon Hampton & Associates
800 K Street, N.W., Suite 720
Washington, DC 20001-8000

webb@delon.com

Dear Mr. Webb:

Thank you so much for taking time from your busy schedule to meet with me on Tuesday. It was very helpful to me to learn so much about the current projects of Delon Hampton & Associates and the career paths of several of your staff. I appreciate your reviewing my portfolio and encouraging my career plans. I also enjoyed meeting Beth Ormond, and am glad to have her suggestions on how I can make the most productive use of my last semester prior to graduation.

Based on what I learned from my visit to your firm and other research I have done, I am very interested in being considered for employment with DHA in the future. I will be available to begin work after I graduate in May 2011. As you saw from my portfolio, I have developed strong skills in the area of historical documentation and this is a good match for the types of projects in which your firm specializes. I have enclosed a copy of my résumé to serve as a reminder of my background, some of which I discussed with you when we met.

During the next few months I will stay in contact with you in hopes that there may be an opportunity to join your firm. Thank you again for your generous help, and I hope you are enjoying a pleasant holiday.

Sincerely,
Kristin Watts
23 Roanoke Street
Charleston, SC 29401
(843) 555-1123
kwatts@yahoo.com

(E-mail version of course has no handwritten signature, and your

Smarter Résumés: A Passion Driven Job Search

signature block appears below your name at the close.)

REFLECTION NOTES

Smarter Résumés: A Passion Driven Job Search

REFLECTION NOTES

Smarter Résumés: A Passion Driven Job Search

REFLECTION NOTES

Smarter Résumés: A Passion Driven Job Search

REFLECTION NOTES

Smarter Résumés: A Passion Driven Job Search

Chapter 8

HOW TO CHOOSE A JOB

REFERENCE

Smarter Résumés: A Passion Driven Job Search

Chapter 8

HOW TO CHOOSE A JOB REFERENCE

When a hiring manager is trying to decide among candidates, the words of someone familiar with the applicant may tip the scale one way or the other. Are your references providing maximum advantage? Here are a few considerations:

The Wall Street Journal published a list of the qualities an ideal reference should have. To see what they are please read more

- People who you are certain think highly of you.
- People who will take the request seriously and be prepared and thoughtful in their answers, even if you don't have time to brief them beforehand (though building in time for a thorough briefing is a wise idea).
- People who understand the context in which the reference is being given.

- People who will know, intuitively, how to present any of your potential weaknesses as strengths.
- People who express themselves well — either verbally or in writing, depending on which type of reference they will be giving.

Think before you select

Good reference is someone who:

- Wants to see you succeed as much as you do.
- Can clearly articulate your strengths, areas of expertise and development.
- Can think on her feet if asked a tough question.
- Is someone for whom you feel good about being a reference

While several people you know may fit the bill, consider whose position or ability to give pertinent information would be most useful to the prospective employer.

In most instances, companies are looking for professional references - - people you have worked for or with who can comment on your skills and accomplishments. There are occasions when companies want more personal/character references, but you should have at least three or four professional references at your disposal, ideally to include a past manager, a colleague, a subordinate (if appropriate) and perhaps someone from another   team/division who you worked with on a particular project.

Since you are looking for references to be enthusiastic advocates, it also is worth considering who might best convince others of your abilities. "There's nothing worse than a potential employer checking a reference who only answers in monosyllables and provides no detail.

It is wise to avoid anyone with whom you did not have a good working relationship and people whom you worked with years ago who are not up-to-date with your current career endeavors. If you're conducting a secret job search, you might want to think carefully about choosing someone from your current workplace. Make sure the person can be trusted to keep the search confidential.

1. A good reference candidate is someone who has known you at least one year - preferably three. Never use family members as references. Your list of references should include four or five of the following:

- Former and/or current supervisors
- Former Professors
- Colleagues and/or subordinates
- Former customers and/or clients
- Contacts from work-related associations or volunteer work

Keep in mind that even if you don't list a former employer as a reference, they can be contacted and interviewed anyway.

2. A good reference candidate should be someone who reinforces and confirms the details of your résumé and offers positive feedback regarding your work or educational skills and experience.

Ask before you list

Once you have chosen four or five candidates, call them to be sure they are willing to provide a reference for you. If it has been awhile since you have talked to them, take the opportunity to bring them up to speed on what you have been doing and send them a current copy of your résumé. Ask them to clarify their perception of your accomplishments, strengths and weaknesses. If you sense any hesitation in their answers, watch out! A good rule of thumb is if they can't speak candidly with you about your work performance, then you have reason to suspect their opinion may be negative.

Contacting people you'd like to use as a reference before listing them serves several purposes:

- It makes you look professional and courteous.
- It gives them time to prepare and not be caught off-guard by a phone call they didn't expect.
- Their willingness or hesitancy can help you judge whether or not they would make a good reference.

NOTE: Just because someone agrees to give a reference, it does not mean that it will be a good one. "Your former supervisor may have had a different impression than you of the quality of work that you provided ... Or what if your boss felt you left him in the lurch when you quit the company?" Instead of assuming, he suggests having a brief conversation with the potential reference in which you can ask what he thought about you as a professional and what he plans to share.

Keep people in the loop

Prepare your references to support your candidacy by briefing them on your background and career goals. Mattson suggests providing each with a current résumé, access to your LinkedIn profile and information on the best way to get in touch with you.

While it is good to update people occasionally on the status of your search, contact is especially useful when you know a potential employer is about to begin checking references. Discussing the position and pointing out key elements that you are trying to emphasize can help your reference prepare informative answers.

Be sure references can be contacted

Once you've finalized your references, be ready to present them to a prospective employer by creating a one-page list that includes the following for each reference:

1. Person's name
2. Job title
3. Relationship to you (such as co-worker or direct supervisor)
4. Company name
5. Address
6. Contact info (phone number, email address)

Check back with your references from time to time to make sure that contact information has not changed. The best reference in the world becomes useless if he can't be reached.

REFLECTION NOTES

Smarter Résumés: A Passion Driven Job Search

REFLECTION NOTES

Smarter Résumés: A Passion Driven Job Search

REFLECTION NOTES

Smarter Résumés: A Passion Driven Job Search

REFLECTION NOTES

Smarter Résumés: A Passion Driven Job Search

SUMMARY

Smarter Résumés: A Passion Driven Job Search

SUMMARY

If you are unemployed, you can wait for employment with dignity and faith.

1. **Recognize that God is in control, even when it seems He has forgotten you.** I love the words to the Old Testament prophet Habakkuk:

Look around at the nations; look and be amazed! For I am doing something in your own day, something you wouldn't believe even if someone told you about it" **(Habakkuk 1:5, NLT)**.

Often when it seems nothing is happening is when everything is happening behind the scenes. You just can't see it.

Renew your faith in God's quiet, steady providence. A few years ago, my wife and I were waiting on several important family and career developments. To quell my anxiety, I did a study on waiting in the Scriptures. I was amazed to find that every major figure in the Bible was forced to wait long periods of time before God brought them to a place of success.

2. **Redeem your time in the waiting room of life.** A few years ago, my wife endured some terrible health challenges. So I've literally spent hours in waiting rooms all over Chicagoland. This was before the age

of iPhones, so I was forced to read three-year old magazines with outdated information. I hated that.

We often do that in our own waiting periods. So anxious are we for that "next step," we languish in despair. But James 1:4 reminds us to "let patience have her perfect work."

Times of uncertainty and doubt are useful periods in which we can draw into God, hone our skills and prepare for the time when that big promotion comes.

Reach out to others and volunteer at a school or volunteer as a way of giving during your time of need.

The Bible tells us to work and not be slothful. Many of us jokingly wish we would inherit some large sum of money so that we no longer have to work. We dream of a life of leisure and not having to daily go to the office, fight the traffic, deal with work-related problems, or cook dinner after returning late. But the Bible tells us differently about work. It tells us that we are all meant to work while we are able. You'll discover that work actually gives you a higher quality of life even if it wears you out. Let's look at the topic of work in the Bible.

The Bible tells us that work was God's plan from the very beginning. Genesis 2:15 (NIV) tells us that even before sin entered into the world, God put Adam and Eve in the garden to look after it. After Adam and Eve sinned and were driven out of the Garden of Eden, they were still told that they would work but it would be much harder work. **Genesis 3:17-19 (NIV)** gives a somewhat unattractive picture of work after God's curse on mankind because weeds were introduced into the picture. Weeds make a person's work much harder.

The Apostle Paul was a strong believer in the work ethic. In fact, Paul was a New Testament evangelist and church planter but he still maintained his secular profession as a tentmaker. In **2 Thessalonians 3:7-10 (NIV)**, Paul explains to the church how he did not want to burden them with the extra expense of his visits so he worked. He petitioned to the church to follow his example of avoiding idleness and told the church in Thessalonica that if anyone does not work, the same should not eat.

The Bible presents the ant as a model for wisdom. A person who is hard-working is considered wise like the ant in the Bible. The passage in **Proverbs 6:6-11 (NIV)** describes the ant and how each day it gathers what it needs for sustenance with no one to tell it what to do. The passage ends with a warning of how slothfulness leads to poverty.

The Bible describes how the slothful person will do nothing to prevent poverty. In the Book of Proverbs, the slothful person is described as one who likes sleep. In **Proverbs 6:9-11 (NIV)**, the slothful person likes to sleep just a little longer unawares of a robber who is quietly taking away everything he has. This description is analogous to those who might sleep or do other lazy activities in the midst of their troubles. For example, a person might lose his or her job and spend the time after the job loss sleeping until noon instead of looking for work. This same person never finds a job and financial troubles accumulate.

Work with perseverance prevents much more than poverty. For instance, it prevents waste or the wasting of opportunities (this is especially important in economically hard times). In **Proverbs 12:27 (NIV)**, we are told of the person who will not work to clean what he hunted for the day and it just goes to waste. Imagine working to achieve some goal yet not fully enjoying its fruits because you won't do the final steps. It's like going to 3 and one-half years of college and dropping out in the very last semester. Of course there are valid reasons students have to drop out of college but this is the person who never returns to finish what he or she started. All the work up to that point goes to waste.

There are ways of thinking that create self motivation. Know that you are a genius! Use your imagination to create and achieve things that worriers never dream of achieving. Use it to create reality. Have a central purpose of life. Create a vision of who you want to be and live in that picture as if it were already true. Be clear and specific. Don't let your goal be too small or vague. It will not be reached if it fails to excite your imagination. Set a large and specific power goal a dream that drives you to achieve all the smaller goals or steps along the way. A goal without action is a daydream. Break your power goal down to smaller goals. Making small attainable goals and keeping a record of when you attain them will build your self-confidence and reassure you that you are making progress.

Make each day a masterpiece! Today is your whole life. Life is now - not later on. Most of us do not focus because we are constantly trying to think of too many things at once. Focus on what you want and it will come into your life. Focus each day on what you are doing, not on the past or on the future. Focus on now. Don't give in to fear! Fear kills us over and over again.

After you have successfully completed these critical steps to finding your job, whether paid or volunteer, ensure that it will be a pleasant experience. During your first few weeks or months you will go through an orientation and probation period. If you are not getting feedback from your employer, request it. Ask your supervisor or team leader about your strengths and your weaknesses. Take advantage of the feedback to learn how you can improve your performance on the job. You are showing that you would like to meet their needs and are eager to fit into the organization. As you become more comfortable, any initial nervousness will subside. You will also be developing the good work habits that future employers want.

Doing good to others is good for the soul, says the Bible. Even when others may do harm to you or treat you badly, it is important to treat everyone with love. **Luke 6:27** says: "But I say unto you which hear, love your enemies, do good to them which hate you." It also states in Romans 12:20 the following: "Therefore if thine enemy hunger, feed him; if he thirst, give him drink: for in so doing thou shalt heap coals of fire on his head." This means that we should do good for others regardless of how they treat us. This is crucial for people who believe the Bible holds truth. It makes you feel righteous as you realize that no matter what happens, you did what you felt was right. In the end, our ultimate benefit is going to heaven.

Pray daily for the right doors to open, favor, and wisdom to develop your emotional intelligence and your sensitivity to the truth. Trust the God in you and while conducting your job search, consider entry-level positions, shadowing, and volunteering.

Smarter Résumés: A Passion Driven Job Search

REFERENCES

References

Angus, J., 2005, 08 22, Seeing the Future with Business Intelligence, InfoWorld, pp. 25-28.

Ellsworth,2000, p. 2; Cohen, 1999; Desruisseaux, 1999b; Coleman; 2000a, p. 10 .

Educational Technology Services (ETS) 2009 Annual Report. Mara Hancock, Educational Technology Services, April 23, 2010.

Ellsworth D. 2000. Seasonal CO_2 assimilation and stomatal limitations in a *Pinus taeda* canopy with varying climate. *Tree Physiology* 20:435-444.

Ferrett, S. Peak Performance, 1997.

Gardner, H., The Unschooled Mind: How Children Think and How Schools Should Teach, Basic.

Haggarty, B., Nurturing Intelligences, Addison-Wesley, Lazar, D., Seven Ways of Learning, Skylight Press.

Herman, Roger E. and Gioia, Joyce L. (2000): How to Become an Employer of Choice
Oakhill Press, Winchester, VA.

Marks-Tarlow, T., Creativity Inside Out, Addison-Wesley.

Milliron, 1999, p. 26; Quick, 2000; Internet Council, 1999; Jupiter Communications, May 2000; Silver   Creek Communications, LLC, 2000; Technology Futures, Inc., March 2000.

Peters, 1994, p. 1). Koch concurs with Peters that it's a knowledge age and more attention will be paid to individual specialness or brand (Koch, 1998, p. 3).

Quick, and Lieb, 2001, p. 41; The National Alliance of Business (NAB), 1999, p. 2.

Robert K. Cooper; Ayman Sawaf: Executive Eq: Emotional Intelligence in Leadership and Organizations. **Putnam Pub Group**, USA, 1997.

Roger Herman and Joyce Gioia, Lean and Meaningful: A New Culture for Corporate America
Oakhill Press, Greensboro, NC, 1998.

Spranger, Eduard (1928) Types of Men.

Swanson, and Hurd, p. 1; Herman and Gioia, 1998, p. 1; The environment analysis report in RSCCD's Master Plan, 2000b.

The Secretary's Commission on Achieving Necessary Skills. *Learning a Living: A Blueprint for High Performance.* A SCANS Report for America 2000. U.S. Department of Labor, 1992.

Teaching the SCANS Competencies. U.S. Department of Labor, 1993.

What Work Requires of Schools. A SCANS Report for America 2000. U.S. Department of Labor, 1992.

Smarter Résumés: A Passion Driven Job Search

RELEVANT SCRIPTURES

Matthew 6:33
But seek first the kingdom of God and his righteousness, and all these things will be added to you.

Philippians 3:13-14
Brothers, I do not consider that I have made it my own. But one thing I do: forgetting what lies behind and straining forward to what lies ahead, I press on toward the goal for the prize of the upward call of God in Christ Jesus.

Deuteronomy 28:1-68
"And if you faithfully obey the voice of the Lord your God, being careful to do all his commandments that I command you today, the Lord your God will set you high above all the nations of the earth. And all these blessings shall come upon you and overtake you, if you obey the voice of the Lord your God. Blessed shall you be in the city, and blessed shall you be in the field. Blessed shall be the fruit of your womb and the fruit of your ground and the fruit of your cattle, the increase of your herds and the young of your flock. Blessed shall be your basket and your kneading bowl. ...

Hebrews 13:8
Jesus Christ is the same yesterday and today and forever.

Luke 10:27
And he answered, "You shall love the Lord your God with all your heart and with all your soul and with all your strength and with all your mind, and your neighbor as yourself."

Smarter Résumés: A Passion Driven Job Search

Leviticus 26:1-46

"You shall not make idols for yourselves or erect an image or pillar, and you shall not set up a figured stone in your land to bow down to it, for I am the Lord your God. You shall keep my Sabbaths and reverence my sanctuary: I am the Lord. "If you walk in my statutes and observe my commandments and do them, then I will give you your rains in their season, and the land shall yield its increase, and the trees of the field shall yield their fruit. Your threshing shall last to the time of the grape harvest, and the grape harvest shall last to the time for sowing. And you shall eat your bread to the full and dwell in your land securely. ...

Psalm 46:1

To the choirmaster. Of the Sons of Korah. According to Alamoth. A Song. God is our refuge and strength, a very present help in trouble.

Exodus 22:1-31

"If a man steals an ox or a sheep, and kills it or sells it, he shall repay five oxen for an ox, and four sheep for a sheep. If a thief is found breaking in and is struck so that he dies, there shall be no bloodguilt for him, but if the sun has risen on him, there shall be bloodguilt for him. He shall surely pay. If he has nothing, then he shall be sold for his theft. If the stolen beast is found alive in his possession, whether it is an ox or a donkey or a sheep, he shall pay double. "If a man causes a field or vineyard to be grazed over, or lets his beast loose and it feeds in another man's field, he shall make restitution from the best in his own field and in his own vineyard. ...

Exodus 20:1-26

And God spoke all these words, saying, "I am the Lord your God, who brought you out of the land of Egypt, out of the house of slavery. "You shall have no other gods before me. "You shall not make for yourself a carved image, or any likeness of anything that is in heaven above, or that is in the earth beneath, or that is in the water under the earth. You shall not bow down to them or serve them, for I the Lord your God am a

Smarter Résumés: A Passion Driven Job Search

jealous God, visiting the iniquity of the fathers on the children to the third and the fourth generation of those who hate me, ...

Genesis 4:1-26
Now Adam knew Eve his wife, and she conceived and bore Cain, saying, "I have gotten a man with the help of the Lord." And again, she bore his brother Abel. Now Abel was a keeper of sheep, and Cain a worker of the ground. In the course of time Cain brought to the Lord an offering of the fruit of the ground, and Abel also brought of the firstborn of his flock and of their fat portions. And the Lord had regard for Abel and his offering, but for Cain and his offering he had no regard. So Cain was very angry, and his face fell. ...

2 Timothy 3:16-17
All Scripture is breathed out by God and profitable for teaching, for reproof, for correction, and for training in righteousness, that the man of God may be competent, equipped for every good work.

1 Timothy 5:8
But if anyone does not provide for his relatives, and especially for members of his household, he has denied the faith and is worse than an unbeliever.

1 Corinthians 10:1-33
For I want you to know, brothers, that our fathers were all under the cloud, and all passed through the sea, and all were baptized into Moses in the cloud and in the sea, and all ate the same spiritual food, and all drank the same spiritual drink. For they drank from the spiritual Rock that followed them, and the Rock was Christ. Nevertheless, with most of them God was not pleased, for they were overthrown in the wilderness. ...

Romans 13:4
For he is God's servant for your good. But if you do wrong, be afraid, for

Smarter Résumés: A Passion Driven Job Search

he does not bear the sword in vain. For he is the servant of God, an avenger who carries out God's wrath on the wrongdoer.

John 14:15
"If you love me, you will keep my commandments.

Luke 10:30-37
Jesus replied, "A man was going down from Jerusalem to Jericho, and he fell among robbers, who stripped him and beat him and departed, leaving him half dead. Now by chance a priest was going down that road, and when he saw him he passed by on the other side. So likewise a Levite, when he came to the place and saw him, passed by on the other side. But a Samaritan, as he journeyed, came to where he was, and when he saw him, he had compassion. He went to him and bound up his wounds, pouring on oil and wine. Then he set him on his own animal and brought him to an inn and took care of him. ...

Luke 2:1-20
In those days a decree went out from Caesar Augustus that all the world should be registered. This was the first registration when Quirinius was governor of Syria. And all went to be registered, each to his own town. And Joseph also went up from Galilee, from the town of Nazareth, to Judea, to the city of David, which is called Bethlehem, because he was of the house and lineage of David, to be registered with Mary, his betrothed, who was with child. ...

Matthew 26:52-54
Then Jesus said to him, "Put your sword back into its place. For all who take the sword will perish by the sword. Do you think that I cannot appeal to my Father, and he will at once send me more than twelve legions of angels? But how then should the Scriptures be fulfilled, that it must be so?"

Matthew 5:1-48

Seeing the crowds, he went up on the mountain, and when he sat down, his disciples came to him. And he opened his mouth and taught them, saying: "Blessed are the poor in spirit, for theirs is the kingdom of heaven. "Blessed are those who mourn, for they shall be comforted. "Blessed are the meek, for they shall inherit the earth. ...

Matthew 4:1-25

Then Jesus was led up by the Spirit into the wilderness to be tempted by the devil. And after fasting forty days and forty nights, he was hungry. And the tempter came and said to him, "If you are the Son of God, command these stones to become loaves of bread." But he answered, "It is written, "'Man shall not live by bread alone, but by every word that comes from the mouth of God.'" Then the devil took him to the holy city and set him on the pinnacle of the temple ...

Proverbs 25:26

Like a muddied spring or a polluted fountain is a righteous man who gives way before the wicked.

2 Chronicles 17:1-19

Jehoshaphat his son reigned in his place and strengthened himself against Israel. He placed forces in all the fortified cities of Judah and set garrisons in the land of Judah, and in the cities of Ephraim that Asa his father had captured. The Lord was with Jehoshaphat, because he walked in the earlier ways of his father David. He did not seek the Baals, but sought the God of his father and walked in his commandments, and not according to the practices of Israel. Therefore the Lord established the kingdom in his hand. And all Judah brought tribute to Jehoshaphat, and he had great riches and honor. ...

Deuteronomy 28:47-48

Because you did not serve the Lord your God with joyfulness and gladness of heart, because of the abundance of all things, therefore you shall serve your enemies whom the Lord will send against you, in hunger and thirst, in nakedness, and lacking everything. And he will put a yoke of iron on your neck until he has destroyed you.

Exodus 22:2-3
If a thief is found breaking in and is struck so that he dies, there shall be no bloodguilt for him, but if the sun has risen on him, there shall be bloodguilt for him. He shall surely pay. If he has nothing, then he shall be sold for his theft.

1 Timothy 2:4
Who desires all people to be saved and to come to the knowledge of the truth.

Romans 12:19
Beloved, never avenge yourselves, but leave it to the wrath of God, for it is written, "Vengeance is mine, I will repay, says the Lord."

John 14:26
But the Helper, the Holy Spirit, whom the Father will send in my name, he will teach you all things and bring to your remembrance all that I have said to you.

Luke 22:36
He said to them, "But now let the one who has a moneybag take it, and likewise a knapsack. And let the one who has no sword sell his cloak and buy one.

Mark 7:1-37
Now when the Pharisees gathered to him, with some of the scribes who had come from Jerusalem, they saw that some of his disciples ate with hands that were defiled, that is, unwashed. (For the Pharisees and all the Jews do not eat unless they wash their hands, holding to the tradition of the elders, and when they come from the marketplace, they do not eat unless they wash. And there are many other traditions that they observe,

such as the washing of cups and pots and copper vessels and dining couches.) And the Pharisees and the scribes asked him, "Why do your disciples not walk according to the tradition of the elders, but eat with defiled hands?" ...

Matthew 5:38-39
"You have heard that it was said, 'An eye for an eye and a tooth for a tooth.' But I say to you, Do not resist the one who is evil. But if anyone slaps you on the right cheek, turn to him the other also.

Psalm 144:1
Of David. Blessed be the Lord, my rock, who trains my hands for war, and my fingers for battle;

Exodus 21:24-25
Eye for eye, tooth for tooth, hand for hand, foot for foot, burn for burn, wound for wound, stripe for stripe.

Genesis 9:5-6
And for your lifeblood I will require a reckoning: from every beast I will require it and from man. From his fellow man I will require a reckoning for the life of man. "Whoever sheds the blood of man, by man shall his blood be shed, for God made man in his own image.

3 John 1:2
Beloved, I pray that all may go well with you and that you may be in good health, as it goes well with your soul.

1 John 4:1
Beloved, do not believe every spirit, but test the spirits to see whether they are from God, for many false prophets have gone out into the world.

1 Peter 5:8
Be sober-minded; be watchful. Your adversary the devil prowls around like a roaring lion, seeking someone to devour.

Colossians 2:8
See to it that no one takes you captive by philosophy and empty deceit, according to human tradition, according to the elemental spirits of the world, and not according to Christ.

Ephesians 6:17
And take the helmet of salvation, and the sword of the Spirit, which is the word of God,

Romans 10:9
Because, if you confess with your mouth that Jesus is Lord and believe in your heart that God raised him from the dead, you will be saved.

Matthew 22:37-38
And he said to him, "You shall love the Lord your God with all your heart and with all your soul and with all your mind. This is the great and first commandment.

Matthew 15:1-39
Then Pharisees and scribes came to Jesus from Jerusalem and said, "Why do your disciples break the tradition of the elders? For they do not wash their hands when they eat." He answered them, "And why do you break the commandment of God for the sake of your tradition? For God commanded, 'Honor your father and your mother,' and, 'Whoever reviles father or mother must surely die.' But you say, 'If anyone tells his father or his mother, "What you would have gained from me is given to God," ...

Matthew 5:19
Therefore whoever relaxes one of the least of these commandments and

teaches others to do the same will be called least in the kingdom of heaven, but whoever does them and teaches them will be called great in the kingdom of heaven.

Matthew 4:7
Jesus said to him, "Again it is written, 'You shall not put the Lord your God to the test.'"

Malachi 3:6
"For I the Lord do not change; therefore you, O children of Jacob, are not consumed.

Nehemiah 4:17-18
Who were building on the wall. Those who carried burdens were loaded in such a way that each labored on the work with one hand and held his weapon with the other. And each of the builders had his sword strapped at his side while he built. The man who sounded the trumpet was beside me.

2 Chronicles 17:10
And the fear of the Lord fell upon all the kingdoms of the lands that were around Judah, and they made no war against Jehoshaphat.

1 Samuel 25:13
And David said to his men, "Every man strap on his sword!" And every man of them strapped on his sword. David also strapped on his sword. And about four hundred men went up after David, while two hundred remained with the baggage.

1 Samuel 13:22-23
So on the day of the battle there was neither sword nor spear found in the hand of any of the people with Saul and Jonathan, but Saul and Jonathan his son had them. And the garrison of the Philistines went out to the pass of Michmash.

1 Samuel 13:19-20

Now there was no blacksmith to be found throughout all the land of Israel, for the Philistines said, "Lest the Hebrews make themselves swords or spears." But every one of the Israelites went down to the Philistines to sharpen his plowshare, his mattock, his axe, or his sickle,

1 Samuel 8:11

He said, "These will be the ways of the king who will reign over you: he will take your sons and appoint them to his chariots and to be his horsemen and to run before his chariots.

Numbers 1:3

From twenty years old and upward, all in Israel who are able to go to war, you and Aaron shall list them, company by company.

John 18:1-40

When Jesus had spoken these words, he went out with his disciples across the Kidron Valley, where there was a garden, which he and his disciples entered. Now Judas, who betrayed him, also knew the place, for Jesus often met there with his disciples. So Judas, having procured a band of soldiers and some officers from the chief priests and the Pharisees, went there with lanterns and torches and weapons. Then Jesus, knowing all that would happen to him, came forward and said to them, "Whom do you seek?" They answered him, "Jesus of Nazareth." Jesus said to them, "I am he." Judas, who betrayed him, was standing with them. ...

Luke 2:1-52

In those days a decree went out from Caesar Augustus that all the world should be registered. This was the first registration when Quirinius was governor of Syria. And all went to be registered, each to his own town. And Joseph also went up from Galilee, from the town of Nazareth, to Judea, to the city of David, which is called Bethlehem, because he was of the house and lineage of David, to be registered with Mary, his betrothed, who was with child. ...

Numbers 31:3

So Moses spoke to the people, saying, "Arm men from among you for the war, that they may go against Midian to execute the Lord's vengeance on Midian.

James 2:1-7

My brothers, show no partiality as you hold the faith in our Lord Jesus Christ, the Lord of glory. For if a man wearing a gold ring and fine clothing comes into your assembly, and a poor man in shabby clothing also comes in, and if you pay attention to the one who wears the fine clothing and say, "You sit here in a good place," while you say to the poor man, "You stand over there," or, "Sit down at my feet," have you not then made distinctions among yourselves and become judges with evil thoughts? Listen, my beloved brothers, has not God chosen those who are poor in the world to be rich in faith and heirs of the kingdom, which he has promised to those who love him? ...

Philippians 2:2

Complete my joy by being of the same mind, having the same love, being in full accord and of one mind.

Hebrews 13:5

Keep your life free from love of money, and be content with what you have, for he has said, "I will never leave you nor forsake you."

1 Corinthians 12:28

And God has appointed in the church first apostles, second prophets, third teachers, then miracles, then gifts of healing, helping, administrating, and various kinds of tongues.

Jeremiah 23:3-4

Then I will gather the remnant of my flock out of all the countries where I have driven them, and I will bring them back to their fold, and they shall be fruitful and multiply. I will set shepherds over them who will care for them, and they shall fear no more, nor be dismayed, neither shall any be missing, declares the Lord.

Exodus 40:1-16

The Lord spoke to Moses, saying, "On the first day of the first month you shall erect the tabernacle of the tent of meeting. And you shall put in it the ark of the testimony, and you shall screen the ark with the veil. And you shall bring in the table and arrange it, and you shall bring in the lamp stand and set up its lamps. And you shall put the golden altar for incense before the ark of the testimony, and set up the screen for the door of the tabernacle. ...

Genesis 1:7

And God made the expanse and separated the waters that were under the expanse from the waters that were above the expanse. And it was so.

Genesis 19:1-38

The two angels came to Sodom in the evening, and Lot was sitting in the gate of Sodom. When Lot saw them, he rose to meet them and bowed himself with his face to the earth and said, "My lords, please turn aside to your servant's house and spend the night and wash your feet. Then you may rise up early and go on your way." They said, "No; we will spend the night in the town square." But he pressed them strongly; so they turned aside to him and entered his house. And he made them a feast and baked unleavened bread, and they ate. But before they lay down, the men of the city, the men of Sodom, both young and old, all the people to the last man, surrounded the house. And they called to Lot, "Where are the men who came to you tonight? Bring them out to us, that we may know them." ...

1 Timothy 6:10

For the love of money is a root of all kinds of evils. It is through this craving that some have wandered away from the faith and pierced themselves with many pangs.

1 Corinthians 6:9-11

Or do you not know that the unrighteous will not inherit the kingdom of God? Do not be deceived: neither the sexually immoral, nor idolaters, nor adulterers, nor men who practice homosexuality, nor thieves, nor the greedy, nor drunkards, nor revilers, nor swindlers will inherit the kingdom of God. And such were some of you. But you were washed, you were sanctified, you were justified in the name of the Lord Jesus Christ and by the Spirit of our God.

Matthew 28:1-20

Now after the Sabbath, toward the dawn of the first day of the week, Mary Magdalene and the other Mary went to see the tomb. And behold, there was a great earthquake, for an angel of the Lord descended from heaven and came and rolled back the stone and sat on it. His appearance was like lightning, and his clothing white as snow. And for fear of him the guards trembled and became like dead men. But the angel said to the women, "Do not be afraid, for I know that you seek Jesus who was crucified. ...

Matthew 6:24

"No one can serve two masters, for either he will hate the one and love the other, or he will be devoted to the one and despise the other. You cannot serve God and money.

Isaiah 1:1-31

The vision of Isaiah the son of Amoz, which he saw concerning Judah and Jerusalem in the days of Uzziah, Jotham, Ahaz, and Hezekiah, kings of Judah. Hear, O heavens, and give ear, O earth; for the Lord has spoken: "Children have I reared and brought up, but they have rebelled against me. The ox knows its owner, and the donkey its master's crib, but Israel does not know, my people do not understand." Ah, sinful nation, a people laden with iniquity, offspring of evildoers, children who deal corruptly! They have forsaken the Lord, they have despised the Holy One of Israel, they are utterly estranged. Why will you still be struck down? Why will you continue to rebel? The whole head is sick, and the whole heart faint. ...

1 Kings 14:24
And there were also male cult prostitutes in the land. They did according to all the abominations of the nations that the Lord drove out before the people of Israel.

Deuteronomy 23:17-18
"None of the daughters of Israel shall be a cult prostitute, and none of the sons of Israel shall be a cult prostitute. You shall not bring the fee of a prostitute or the wages of a dog into the house of the Lord your God in payment for any vow, for both of these are an abomination to the Lord your God.

Genesis 2:24
Therefore a man shall leave his father and his mother and hold fast to his wife, and they shall become one flesh.

Genesis 1:27
So God created man in his own image, in the image of God he created him; male and female he created them.

Hebrews 13:4
Let marriage be held in honor among all, and let the marriage bed be undefiled, for God will judge the sexually immoral and adulterous.

2 Timothy 3:16
All Scripture is breathed out by God and profitable for teaching, for reproof, for correction, and for training in righteousness,

Romans 1:26-27

For this reason God gave them up to dishonorable passions. For their women exchanged natural relations for those that are contrary to nature; and the men likewise gave up natural relations with women and were consumed with passion for one another, men committing shameless acts with men and receiving in themselves the due penalty for their error.

John 8:16

Yet even if I do judge, my judgment is true, for it is not I alone who judge, but I and the Father who sent me.

Leviticus 20:13

If a man lies with a male as with a woman, both of them have committed an abomination; they shall surely be put to death; their blood is upon them.

Leviticus 18:22

You shall not lie with a male as with a woman; it is an abomination.

Smarter Résumés: A Passion Driven Job Search

REFLECTION NOTES

Smarter Résumés: A Passion Driven Job Search

REFLECTION NOTES

Smarter Résumés: A Passion Driven Job Search

REFLECTION NOTES

Smarter Résumés: A Passion Driven Job Search

REFLECTION NOTES

Smarter Résumés: A Passion Driven Job Search

REFLECTION NOTES

Smarter Résumés: A Passion Driven Job Search

REFLECTION NOTES

REFLECTION NOTES

Smarter Résumés: A Passion Driven Job Search

REFLECTION NOTES

REFLECTION NOTES

Smarter Résumés: A Passion Driven Job Search

REFLECTION NOTES

REFLECTION NOTES

Smarter Résumés: A Passion Driven Job Search

REFLECTION NOTES

REFLECTION NOTES

Smarter Résumés: A Passion Driven Job Search

REFLECTION NOTES

REFLECTION NOTES

REFLECTION NOTES

REFLECTION NOTES

Smarter Résumés: A Passion Driven Job Search

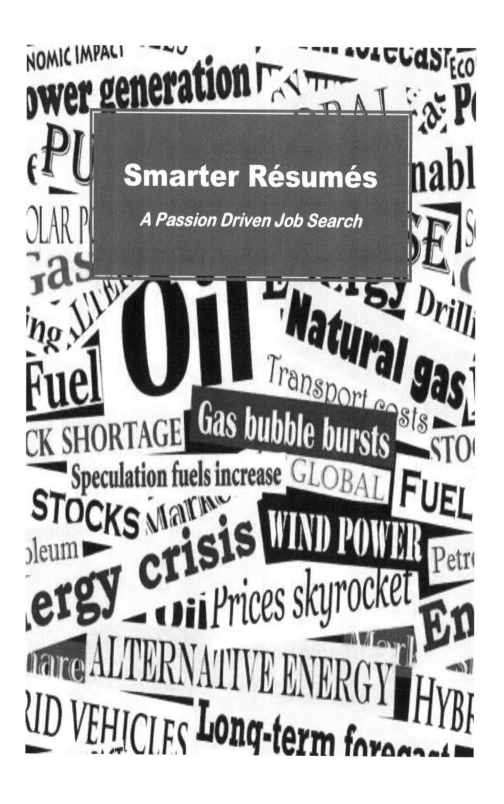

Smarter Résumés: A Passion Driven Job Search

Smarter Résumés

A Passion Driven Job Search

By Dr. Hester Young

248

Smarter Résumés: A Passion Driven Job Search

Smarter Résumés

A Passion Driven Job Search

By Dr. Hester Young

Smarter Résumés: A Passion Driven Job Search

251

Smarter Résumés: A Passion Driven Job Search

Smarter Résumés: A Passion Driven Job Search

Smarter Résumés: A Passion Driven Job Search

255

Smarter Résumés: A Passion Driven Job Search

Smarter Résumés: A Passion Driven Job Search

257

Smarter Résumés: A Passion Driven Job Search

Smarter Résumés: A Passion Driven Job Search